PATTERNS OF THE *Heart*

Discernment in Choosing a Potential Spouse

RUSSELYN L. WILLIAMS

Copyright © 2019 Russelyn L. Williams

THE HOLY BIBLE, NEW INTERNATIONAL VERSION®, NIV® Copyright © 1973, 1978, 1984, 2011 by Biblica, Inc.® Used by permission. All rights reserved worldwide.

Scripture quotations marked (NLT) are taken from the Holy Bible, New Living Translation, copyright © 1996, 2004, 2007, 2013, 2015 by Tyndale House Foundation. Used by permission of Tyndale House Publishers, Inc., Carol Stream, Illinois 60188. All rights reserved.

CONTENTS

Introduction 5

Chapter 1: How Do I Know If I'm Whole? 13
Chapter 2: Good Questions to Ask a Potential Spouse 25
Chapter 3: Breaking Down Questions 1 through 6 27
Chapter 4: Vision of Marriage Question 35
Chapter 5: Part II Answers to Questions Cont'd 50
Chapter 6: Avoid Dating Down 56
Chapter 7: Case Studies 65
Chapter 8: Nuggets 95

INTRODUCTION

This book was written with people like me in mind, those who find it hard to meet someone who matches their maturity level or, at the very least, a committed desire to grow in Christ. Too often, we judge a person's character by how they appear. If a person is too attractive, we assume they can't be bout it bout it for the Lord. Or, if a person looks the part, we assume they are all in, just like us, without allowing time and circumstance to qualify them.

This book is also for those who aren't sure what to expect in a relationship or how a Biblically sound relationship should look. This book can be used as a roadmap to assist in navigating dating, courtship, and a well-constructed personal vision for a healthy and God-centered relationship.

This book provides open-ended questions that reveals more than the surface of what may be in a person's heart. The Bible says that out of the abundance of the heart, the mouth speaks. Sometimes, in general conversation, God will allow a potential to tell on him/her self—saving the other party time and energy.

On other occasions, a person may have all the right answers, but the fruit, meaning their consistent actions, do not line up with what's being said. The only way to know if what they're saying and doing is correct, according to God's standard, is to know the Word of God.

This book provides 10 questions to ask a potential spouse or 10 questions to simply ponder and observe within a person's actions. It also gives 10 explanations of why these questions are important and what to look for in the answers and/or as we observe a person. Additionally, this book offers scripture confirming each explanation. When we base our lives on rightly dividing the Word of God, we cannot go wrong.

Instead of interrogating a potential mate with these questions, I would encourage you to ask naturally and in an appropriate setting. You might even put the questions into your own words, using your communication style. In some cases, it may not even be necessary to ask; it may be more feasible to simply observe behavior and listen for voluntary information. I believe it's good for women to allow the man to lead the discussion. Often, when a man is pursuing a young lady, he is so excited to be in her presence, that he continually talks, telling her all about himself.

Initially, we really don't need to ask very many questions. As a matter of fact, I believe it's wise for women not to share too much about ourselves initially so the man shares who he is and what he's about authentically. We don't want him to attempt to pattern himself based on what he thinks we want from our conversation. This causes this relationship to become an act instead of a naturally evolving God-connection.

A man can only act for so long; eventually, his true colors must show, which is why we have to remain patient while guarding our hearts and allowing ourselves to be pursued. Being content with who we are in Christ and where God has us currently will help us with guarding our hearts. This way, we aren't so emotionally invested in the relationship that we aren't willing to address important red-flags. Men should also guard their hearts while getting to know a woman closely and watching her fruit. The questions offered will not only provide great in-depth conversation and a view into the heart, but it will also show us where our hearts are and where are beliefs stand.

So many people get in and out of relationships without a personal standard for themselves. This produces a rocky foundation that invites failure during an attempt to build, which is why we shouldn't date until we're whole and we know ourselves. When we're whole, we don't look for someone else to fill our voids, fix us, or give us what only God can. People who aren't whole are overly needy and prime game for co-dependent relationships.

In co-dependent relationships, the other person relies on his or her partner to fix them or mask an issue that hasn't been dealt with. Often, individuals in co-dependent relationships feel as though they can't function properly without the other person. This is a very dangerous relationship and is simply idolatry. In relationships like this, God often withdraws his hand, except for his grace and mercy, so that the parties can re-focus their attention on him.

Here's what *Mental Health America's* website shares on co-dependent relationships:

> "Co-dependents have low self-esteem and look for anything outside of themselves to make them feel better. They find it hard to "be themselves." Some try to feel better through alcohol, drugs or nicotine - and become addicted. Others may develop com-

pulsive behaviors like workaholism, gambling, or indiscriminate sexual activity.

They have good intentions. They try to take care of a person who is experiencing difficulty, but the caretaking becomes compulsive and defeating. Co-dependents often take on a martyr's role and become "benefactors" to an individual in need."

More on co-dependents from Mental Health America:

"The problem is that these repeated rescue attempts allow the needy individual to continue on a destructive course and to become even more dependent on the unhealthy caretaking of the "benefactor." As this reliance increases, the co-dependent develops a sense of reward and satisfaction from "being needed." When the caretaking becomes compulsive, the co-dependent feels choiceless and helpless in the relationship, but is unable to break away from the cycle of behavior that causes it. Co-dependents view themselves as victims and are attracted to that same weakness in the love and friendship relationships."

A person operating out of a co-dependent relationship will need deliverance from putting his/her trust in man. He/she will need to grow their personal trust in the Lord through trials and tribulations. The Bible says the man who leans to the arm of the flesh is cursed. When we look to man to provide what only God should provide, we set ourselves up to fail.

Additionally, we often stick around when a relationship proves to be unhealthy. I will admit: I used to be in a place where I allowed guys who obviously weren't ready or weren't the one to stick around longer than they should have. The lack of options of godly men my age made me more patient than I should have been with a man who showed me he was not ready, but seemed to be more ready than most. I used to be one who thought I had to make the best of the limited choices I saw. But now, as an older, more mature daughter of God, I'm more confident in the fact that I'm simply rare, just as the Bible says a virtuous woman is. And because I'm rare, my counterpart must also be rare to be a good fit for who God has made me to be.

My husband is probably out there dealing with similar situations that I have. We're both likely fighting the lies of the enemy, the ones that seek to make us feel like we're too one-of-a-kind to be with anyone. However, God's voice is louder, and God has a proven track record. This is how I know that my desire for a spouse will be provided. I simply hide God's word away in my heart as I stand on his promises, I use the wisdom he provides to weed out the wrong guys and I remain open for the right guy.

Here's a consistent prayer I use when I first meet a guy I'm interested in: "Lord, if this is you, open the door. If this is not you, keep the door shut." This prayer is based on the scripture below:

> "These are the words of him who is holy and
> true, who holds the key of David. What he

opens no one can shut, and what he shuts no one can open." - Revelations 3:7 (NIV)

I strongly believe that the key of David is a heart after God. In the Bible, King David was characterized by having a heart after God. He was constantly seeking the Lord regarding all his decisions, and he wanted to please God with his life. He constantly learned to submit himself to the Lord, allowing himself to rest in the fact that God had the best for him and that God's way was perfect, meaning lacking nothing (See Psalms 18:30).

Based on words of prophecy spoken over me and my personal relationship with Christ, I strongly believe there is a door that will open for me, and that's the only door I'm interested in—the door, opportunity, or spouse God has set aside for me. I don't want any other opportunities or doors; I only want what God wants for me. And I can stand on this because this is God's word.

I can be expectant since God's word says that when I seek, I will find. The deal is that I don't want to put so much focus on it that it becomes an idol or stumbling block to me. However, I do need to expect that God will fulfill his Word, and when he does, it will exceed my expectations. As it pertains to relationships, I personally believe that many who turn away from God to seek their own way do so because of unbelief. They simply don't believe that there's someone for them or that they are good enough to attain what God has promised them. I've struggled with this before, and I've overcome. Thankfully, I'm in a new place now.

A large part of being whole is moving past what we see in our lives and instead focusing on what God has said. Getting past the personal voids and inadequacies that cause us to choose what's available right now; instead of what's right for us, will put us in a position of wholeness so that we're able to discern and choose wisely.

In the next chapter, we'll do some self-discovery to determine our current level of wholeness.

CHAPTER 1

How Do I Know If I'm Whole?

When God brings a person to a place of wholeness, he begins to resolve issues, mindsets, and patterns of thinking that stem from unhealthy places. The reason God does this is so that we will walk in his overwhelming peace instead of remaining in a constant state of trying to fix ourselves.

For example: Do you hate men? Why? Where did that mentality come from? What defense mechanisms did that produce within your personality? Have you become bitter because of your perspective? On your journey to wholeness, God brings up all of this stuff to deal with the dirty and hidden parts of our hearts that even we don't see.

"I the LORD search the heart and examine the mind, to reward each person according to their conduct, according to what their deeds deserve." - Jeremiah 17:10 (NIV)

God digs deep into our hearts beginning a deliverance process so our mindsets shift to his way of thinking. This elevates us and prepares us for new heights in God and what He has for us.

Therefore, it's so important to count all joy when going through many temptations; they're preparing us for something.

However, it's easy for us to become unthankful due to the difficulty of the tests, but if we can keep the right perspective with a thankful heart, we'll do well. (See James 1:2-8).

This scripture describes someone in a godly process and the temptation to become unstable in our thinking during that time. The unsteadiness in our thinking reveals what's in our hearts. It reveals when we're double minded, and when we're double minded, we won't receive anything from God. We simply aren't ready yet to steward the next season.

Take the parable about the wine-skins that Jesus gave. He simply said that you cannot pour new wine into old wine-skins because if you do so, the old wine-skins will cause the wine to leak out because they're stretched and worn. Therefore, God has to create a new wine-skin that can handle the new wine. This is symbolic for the new move of God or the direction He's taking us in. We cannot properly steward the next season of our lives with an old mindset. God must give us a new mindset causing us to grow in maturity for the specific purpose He has for us. In this sense, we become new like the wine-skins.

We cannot compare ourselves to someone who's married and assume they are more mature than us or are married because they have dotted Is or crossed Ts that we haven't. Other people's purposes simply aren't ours. God does things according to His will. The Bible says that God disburses gifts to men according to his will (1 Corinthians 12:11). Your purpose may require a greater level of maturity than others because you have a greater level of stewardship on your life. Don't compare yourself or your personal wholeness to others. Being in competition about our current circumstances as it relates to others is another sign that we aren't yet whole in our thinking and how we see ourselves.

What This Looked Like for Me

God set me on a deliverance course, revealing where the roots of me being bitter and feeling let down by men came from. In my book, "The Single Christian Woman's Guide," I briefly discussed how God delivered me from bitterness and wrong thinking concerning men. One day, an older woman broke down the man's role to me very clearly. She said that his role is to provide, protect, and act as priest. The priest provides identity and has an intimate connection with God. She asked if my father and the men in my life provided for me, and I said yes. She asked if they protected me. Again, I said yes. When she asked about the priest, I shared that I felt I had to take on that role for myself to a strong degree.

I had resented the fact that because the men in my life did not fulfill their priestly role, as I desired, I felt uncovered in my mind, will, and emotions. When it came to getting to know men for my personal relationships, I couldn't see myself continuing with a guy who couldn't fulfill the role of priest in my life. I simply refused to go without that from the partner that I'd choose to wed for life. I was upset at men because I had not met anyone who could meet that role.

When I finally met a man, who seemed qualified to meet that role; he didn't want me at all. I had already been questioning whether I was good enough to be pursued, loved, and won by a loving man. I had several unresolved issues, including the fear that I was too spiritual or too into God for a man to even want me. That's what Christian people would tell me. It had gotten to the point where I'd become guarded and wouldn't show people the spiritual side of me unless I felt I could trust them enough to not judge me for being me.

The truth is, I was putting my trust in man to affirm me, tell me I wasn't crazy and that there was nothing wrong with me. I was looking for a man to say that it's okay to want to please God and desire a man who does the same. I wanted a man to say, "I'll walk with you, love you, and cover you. You are worthy of being loved and pursued, and I will show you."

However, God didn't raise me to put my trust in man. Remember, God will allow those who lean to the arm of the flesh to be cursed (Jeremiah 17:5). He wants us to look to Him. During my times of weakness, when I was looking to men, I should have been looking to God to cover me, affirm me, and show me that I'm worthy of love. I should have been thankful that God covered me in such an unconventional way. To expose what was in my heart and where my trust lied, God allowed the disappointment from the gentleman who didn't want me to show me I didn't fully trust the Lord like I thought. I needed to grow in my trusting God to become whole and ready for what He had for me.

In this elevated perspective during my broken season, I began looking at my dad and the other men in my life differently. I was able to appreciate them more, treating them with greater compassion. I saw that my dad performed the role of priest as best as he knew how. It was my dad who made us watch Christian television growing up, and it was him who made us stand up when he caught us falling asleep while watching. He did this without even knowing or fully realizing the freedom and deliverance afforded to him in Christ. The things he did planted seeds in me, preparing me for who I've become today.

I now look at my dad with the utmost respect, despite his flaws. I'd always tried to do this, but sometimes it had been harder than others due to the brokenness in his life and how it affected my family as a whole. However, all in all, things have worked out for our good, just as God promised.

Being compassionate and showing mercy and grace for others, even when they don't do right, is a great character to have during marriage. Marriage is supposed to be a representation of the gospel of Christ. God's grace is enough for us no matter where we are in the process of life, faith, and intimacy with Him. That's the beauty of salvation. The man who comes into this at the end of his life receives the same glorious salvation as the man who came in toward the beginning of his because salvation is not something that's worked for, but given by God's grace toward us (Matthew 20:1-16). And just as God shows us grace through Christ, we ought to also show grace to each other. As a matter of fact, marriage is the husband and wife taking turns reflecting Christ to one another. Remember, Christ forgave us while we were yet in our sins. The husband needs to give his wife grace, forgiving her when she's at fault, and the wife should do the same. In this, the two reflect Christ to one another and the world.

People who don't learn to show grace and mercy to others are very critical and judgmental and often drive people away. Therefore, it's so important to allow God's deliverance process to free us. (Read more about wholeness in my book, "The Wholeness Action Plan").

Making Progress

After God has processed us, He often allows more tests to show us our progress. Then, he begins to flood us with His peace, and we'll notice that we are settled. We're no longer moved by what we see or don't see. We are moved by our trust and reliance on God.

"But blessed is the one who trusts in the Lord, whose confidence is in him. They will be like a tree planted by the water that sends out its roots by the stream. It does not fear when heat comes; its leaves are always green. **It has no worries in a year of drought and never fails to bear fruit.**" – Jeremiah 17:7-8 (NIV)

The bolded section speaks of a person who is no longer moved by what they see. A drought typically signifies there isn't enough of something to go around and that harvest will be short. The person who allows their soul to be at rest by trusting in the Lord won't worry about a drought. She knows her needs will be met by the one who loves her so very much. The person who is whole is full, even in lack. Selah on Jeremiah 17 when you get a chance.

It's interesting because after my perspective began to change, God started showing me there are godly men out there my age. I even began building relationships/friendships with some of them. I was humble and compassionate enough to not judge them for not being healed enough to meet my needs because that wasn't their job. God even brought me closer with the men in my life and showed me how to pray for them even more because I could see their insecurities. I've often had to encourage them more directly regarding their self-doubt.

The focus wasn't on me as much anymore and what I needed when dealing with men, but on operating from a place of wholeness to add to the lives of those God placed around me and to do it without resentment or a perspective of missing something. The truth is we all are broken at times and in need of the ever-loving God.

Even King David, who composed beautiful psalms speaking of God's perfect way and how worthy He is of our trust, had to be processed from a place of brokenness to wholeness. King David dealt with rejection in his home. He wasn't even a consideration for king when the prophet Samuel was sent to his house. God had sent him to hand-pick David, and this was the beginning of God's public proclamation of David's purpose in front of his brothers and father, who had talked down to and despised him. David would have to be humble enough to show grace, during his process of wholeness and preparation for becoming king. This was demonstrated when he served Saul despite Saul's attempt to kill him. David spared Saul's life and continued honoring him as king until he died.

It's implied that these events took place over several years. After David was processed, he was able to recount the below about the Lord:

> "With your help I can advance against a troop;
> with my God I can scale a wall.
> As for God, his way is perfect:
> The Lord's word is flawless;
> he shields all who take refuge in him.
> For who is God besides the Lord?
> And who is the Rock except our God?
> It is God who arms me with strength
> and keeps my way secure." - Psalms 18:29-32 (NIV)

Here is my interpretation of the above scripture, which is my favorite:

By leaning on God, David was able to overcome what was meant to destroy him. However, instead of it destroying him, it made him stronger, reassuring him that he could overcome any obstacle. Additionally, David's revelation of God had increased. Prior to this, there had been times of doubt when David questioned what God was doing, whether He would save him, or if God had made a mistake anointing him as king. Now, he saw God's bigger plan. He recognized that God's way was perfect and flawless all along. The circumstances that had transpired didn't catch God off guard. Instead, He was a refuge for David in process, and David became more secure than he'd ever been. If he hadn't gone through what he did, he wouldn't have known the security and peace that comes from leaning on the Lord.

This is the place God desires us to be as single believers: The place where no matter what transpires, we know that God will keep us secure and take care of us. This is a place of extreme rest and peace in God. Being in this state allows us to depend on Him for what we need instead of placing false burdens on others. It can become very tiring and counter-productive to expect our spouses to fix our insecurities. They aren't equipped to fix them; only God is. Spouses can remind us to look to Christ for that, but they cannot fix us.

Going through the process allows our needs to be fulfilled in Christ. We become steadier when facing the winds of the next season of marriage, promise, and covenant. There will be times where we'll have to fight and stand firm on our foundation to remain successful by God's standards. We can do this more effortlessly when we've been processed into people who have become whole in Christ.

The Bible says that he that is spiritual should be able to evaluate all things, but they themselves cannot be evaluated by others. (1 Corinthians 2:15)

We should have a healthy self-awareness where we aren't judging ourselves harshly, but with grace to ensure we're depending on Christ. We need a genuine level of discernment for where we are and those, we are considering dating.

I've composed a few questions to ponder to determine whether you're walking whole in Christ, or if you're relying on other people/things to do what only God can:

1. Are you allowing unhealthy things and people into intimate parts of your life/heart to fill a void God wants you to trust Him to fill? For example, old boyfriends/girlfriends who aren't leading to what God has for you--situationships and such?
2. What are you doing consistently to show that you love yourself?
3. Do you have healthy boundaries in your life? Or do you regularly let them go to be accepted by others. Would you bend your boundaries to be accepted by pastors, leaders, or notable people, valuing them more than yourself? People often relinquish who they are and their boundaries to be accepted by prominent people because they believe those people make them greater. While honor is always in order, disrespecting our boundaries and who we are isn't a healthy requirement to a relationship. A person who continues in this way, may indicate insecurity and a need for acceptance. Our acceptance should first be affirmed by what Christ says about us. God says we have been accepted in the beloved (Ephesians 1:6.)
4. Are you being led by fear or faith? Fear paralyzes. Faith keeps you moving since you're motivated by God's

promises. Fear produces stagnation due to the fear of not having enough or not attaining what God has promised.

5. Are you consistently having quiet time with the Lord, meditating on God's word?
6. Are you relying more on men and blogs than on Christ?
7. Have you become lazy in seeking the Lord because you're surrounded by others who seek him? You may have become too comfortable, and God might have to give you some tests so you can rely on him.
8. Do you know what God's standard is for your life? Are you willing to suffer or endure discomfort to hold up that standard while trusting in the Lord? When you're at this point, you're willing to lose the things that don't line up with God's standard, knowing that His guidelines will produce something far greater.
9. Are you committed to God's standard no matter what, or will you bend them to be in a relationship?
10. Do you easily give yourself grace when you're at fault? Do you easily give others grace when they're at fault?
11. Are you committed to forgiving others, and are you committed to forgiving yourself?
12. Are you enjoying life where you are, having faith for the future?
13. Are you hating your life right now, focused only on seeking something different for the future?
14. Do you project your insecurities on others? Do you take responsibility for being whole and seeing yourself the way you should—the way God sees you?
15. Is the joy of the Lord your strength or do you find your joy in things, people, and places? It's okay to be

happy and joyful about new experiences and such; that's a part of life. But if that's the main source of your joy, rather than growing in Christ and receiving the covenant of his great inheritance, that's going to be a problem. It will create a roller coaster experience in our emotions, our joy going up and down based on outside situations.

16. Do you speak negatively often? Are you a complainer? Are you unthankful? This person still needs to be in process.
17. Do you often compare yourself to others and where they are in life as opposed to where you are in life?
18. What are some of the unresolved issues in your heart concerning your upbringing? If there are matters in your heart concerning your upbringing, don't run by looking for a new relationship to gloss over them; confront them. Get counseling, pour out your soul to God until you are healed, exchange your perspective for God's, share with a wise mentor.

These are just a few questions to answer honestly by observing yourself and your actions and by God making you aware of things that you may not be conscious of that require healing.

Allow the Lord to prepare you. If it's not a time for you to date, that's okay. Don't feel pressured to date or be in a relationship just because you're a particular age. Date when you're whole and ready. Date when you're firm on your identity in Christ. Until then, endure God's process of making you whole, just like David and I did. As long as you're committed to the Lord, and He's promised you a spouse, your time will come. He will prepare those He has called to marriage. And even after marriage, you'll still need to rely on God as your spouse further prunes you and you further prune him/her. It's important that both parties be committed to the process because it won't always be easy. However, if we can be committed to God's process as single believers, we'll be committed as married believers.

This goes along with the Biblical principle that if we are faithful in little, we'll be faithful in much. Marriage will be the much for us. It will be more responsibility than we have now, and we have to continue to remain faithful in our now season trusting God.

It is also wise to know where you stand concerning the questions in the next section so you'll have a firm understanding, Biblical vision, and foundation when moving forward to pursue a spouse:

"Where there is no vision, the people perish: but he that keepeth the law, happy is he." - Proverbs 29:18 (KJV)

When you go in with a strong vision of who you are and what you have a right to Biblically expect, you have a better chance at avoiding failure. In this way, you'll be whole and well-informed enough to weed out the unsuitable, making room for the one who is for you. It isn't wise to go in any other way.

CHAPTER 2

Good Questions to Ask a Potential Spouse

1.) On a scale of 1-10, how would you rate your current trust in the Lord?
2.) Do you have goals and dreams for your future? Can you tell me about them?
3.) How well do you love yourself? What are some examples of things you do to show that you love yourself?
4.) What are your close friends like?
5.) Do you have people in your inner circle who can tell you the truth about yourself?
6.) How do you deal with disappointment? Can you give an example?
7.) What is your understanding of marriage, practically and spiritually?
8.) What would you say you believe God is doing in your life right now?
9.) What are some things that you practice to maintain discipline in various areas of your life, such as sexuality,

eating habits, the way you spend your time, and money management?

10.) How open are you to correction, and how do you view it? Do you see it as something that can help you grow, or do you see it as a put-down to who you are?

Some Additional Things to Observe in a Potential Spouse

- What is your understanding of grace?
- How merciful are you to yourself and others?
- Do you believe in forgiving quickly? Can you share an example? Have you been tested in this area? If so, how do you feel you did?
- How do you deal with your insecurities? See marriage question for details on how a man can deal with his insecurities.
- What is it that you are looking for something short-term, long-term, marriage?
- What have you learned from your parent's relationship?
- What have you learned from your past relationships?
- Why do you want to be married?

CHAPTER 3

Breaking Down Questions 1 through 6

On a Scale of 1-10, how would you rate your trust in the Lord?

These questions give so much insight about where a believer is in his walk. It can show signs as to how committed he/she is. I've found that just as Christ and his church is a metaphor for a husband and wife; similarly, I can learn a lot about a potential suitor by how he treats his relationship with God. Trust is born out of intimacy. If there's no intimacy, there will be no trust. If there is little intimacy, there will be little trust. A man who hasn't learned how to walk with the Lord in his singleness, trusting in Him, is often a man who seeks to control how everything turns out. And it's the same for a woman who hasn't learned to walk with God. She will use whatever means to control a situation or relationship. Control is a manifestation of insecurity and fear. Insecurity unchecked is an open door to physical and verbal abuse.

If you're dating someone who hasn't learned to trust in the Lord, you have to decide if you have the patience to deal with this. Does the person want to grow, or is the potential suitor simply walking in the flesh, identifying with Christ as having a religious spirit only? You should consider what you may end up dealing with by continuing with the person. He or she may be prideful and unwilling to change. Or, he or she may be stubborn and seeking his or her own way. These could be huge obstacles in a healthy relationship, and it could be excessively draining. You're the only one who will know whether you will have the patience to handle this person. If you operate from a lack of trust in the Lord, you may not find a problem with this. Perhaps you'll grow together with the person, or maybe they'll decide to remain the same while you decide to grow later, and then a wedge grows between the two of you. If you're a person of great depth and trust in the Lord, you'd be in an unequally yoked relationship. If you proceeded with the unequally yoked relationship, you'd have to brace yourself for unnecessary hard times. The choice is yours. What will you choose?

> "Trust in the LORD with all your heart; do not depend on your own understanding. Seek his will in all you do, and he will show you which path to take. Don't be impressed with your own wisdom. instead, fear the LORD and turn away from evil. - Proverbs 3:5-7 (NLT)

Do you have goals & dreams for your future?

This shows good character in a person. Having goals and dreams for his/her future shows diligence, thoughtfulness, and the ability to plan and possibly follow through if the person is taking steps toward his/her future. The Bible clearly says without a vision, my people perish. A vision provides structure, which, in turn provides security, which is an excellent quality to possess. Knowing whether a person has a vision will show you if he or she is somewhat living life with no direction, or if he or she has discipline. It will also show you if a person is a talker or a doer. Many people talk about their dreams and procrastinate, while others take steps learning, and walking by faith until they accomplish their dreams. Which one are you, and which one is your potential suitor? This question might also reveal a person's diligent spirit. If a person is passionate about his/her dreams for the future, he/she may open up and talk about it more, sharing some of the things they've put in place to work toward it. On the other hand, stagnation can also be revealed by the answer to this question. For example, I dated a brother who I had asked this question and he did not know what he was passionate about or his goals. He finally shared that he wanted to attend school for a higher paying position at his job, but he never took any steps toward it. He was one who talked, but did not do. He was one who was stagnant and content to remain in the same place. This was not only seen in his personal career goals, but in other important areas of his life, such as his walk with the Lord, unwillingness to lead as a man, and his inability to grow in general. Stagnation had become a way of life in too many areas of his life. I knew that was not the path God had for me.

> Diligent hands will rule, but laziness ends in forced labor. - Proverbs 12:24 (NIV)

How well do you love yourself? What are some examples of things that you do that show you love yourself?

This is a very important one as it indicates how a person will treat you. The Bible is clear that we are to love our neighbors as we love ourselves. I've noticed that people who hate themselves tend to abuse others and, in some cases, they abuse themselves, too.

Ladies, whether a man loves himself or not is a sign of if he'll treat you the way he should. Ephesians 5 tells men to love their wives as their own bodies, and it goes on to say that no man yet hated his own body. The scripture below is foundational in a healthy relationship with yourself and others, including your potential spouse. He or she should treat you no less lovely than the way they treat themselves.

> "For no man ever yet hated his own flesh; but nourisheth and cherisheth it, even as the Lord the church." - Ephesians 5:29 (KJV)
> Love the Lord your God with all your heart and with all your soul and with all your mind and with all your strength. The second is this: 'Love your neighbor as yourself. There is no commandment greater than these." - Mark 12:30-31(NIV)

What are your close friends like?

Knowing what a potential interest's close friends are like will provide some insight into what your interest is like. The Bible implies, on more than one occasion, that we can influence one another by simply hanging around together. This works in both positive and negative directions. We tend to become like those we hang around most; therefore, learning what a potential mate's close friends are like can provide some insight into what he/she is like. Hopefully, the friendships are influencing him/her for the better and not for the worst. While this can be adjusted if a person is willing, he/she has to be one who welcomes growth and positive change.

> "Walk with the wise and become wise; associate with fools and get in trouble." - Proverbs 13:20 (NLT)

> "Do not be misled: 'Bad company corrupts good character.'" - 1 Corinthians 15:33

> "As iron sharpens iron, so one person sharpens another." - Proverbs 27:17

Do you have people in your inner circle who can tell you the truth about yourself?

The Bible is clear that the truth makes us free, which is why we must become lovers of truth. A lover of truth is a lover of Christ because Christ is truth. Thus, we need friends who can bring us into the truth of Christ's light, which is God's word. We should welcome this into our lives.

"This is the verdict: Light has come into the world, but people loved darkness instead of light because their deeds were evil. Everyone who does evil hates the light, and will not come into the light for fear that their deeds will be exposed." - John 3:19-20 (NIV)

There are some who simply don't want to hear truth. Why? Because they don't want to change their ways. They may associate with Christ, the church, or religion to portray themselves as believers to attract true believers, but one of the marks of being alive in Christ is continually growing. You won't be content staying in sin or in wrong ways of thinking and doing things. The Holy Spirit causes us to transform as we submit to Him. A person who doesn't value others in his/her life telling him/her the truth is comfortable staying the same. They aren't seeking to grow in Christ and in godliness. They are simply seeking to be comfortable. Be very careful around a person who doesn't invite and value the truth from those in their lives.

Also, if a man/woman is the strongest one in their group, he or she needs to expand or switch groups. We all need others to help sharpen us. Get with someone who is willing to sharpen you and be sharpened by you and others.

> "Do not reprove a scoffer, or he will hate you; reprove a wise man, and he will love you." - Proverbs 9:8 (ESV)

Scoffer: someone who jeers or mocks or treats something with contempt or calls out in derision (vocabulary.com); synonyms: jeerer, mocker type, disagreeable person, unpleasant person.

> "And you shall know the truth, and the truth shall make you free." - John 8:32

> "As iron sharpens iron, so one person sharpens another."- Proverbs 27:17

How do you deal with disappointment?

How we respond when things don't go our way reveals our character. A disappointment is not a reason to give up on God, life, family, people, or dreams. How we deal with setbacks show our resiliency or lack thereof. This can be a great conversation with potential partners because it can uncover patterns we've grown in since the last disappointment or the hardness that we've developed because of it. We don't need to find this out so we can judge a person, but to see how he/she deals with life. What are his/her coping mechanisms? Are they healthy, leading to wholeness, or unhealthy leading to more brokenness? Someone once said broken people break people, but also, whole people heal people. If a person knows how to properly heal from disappointment, they can become a healing agent to others. On the contrary, if a person allows themselves to become hard due to disappointment, they can make things very uncomfortable for those around. Do your due diligence to find out if you have the grace to deal with someone who doesn't know how to deal with disappointment well. Additionally, learn how to better deal with it yourself. What did you learn about yourself and coping skills from your last disappointment? Is the person you're dating willing to learn and grow concerning how he/she deals with disappointment?

"Hope deferred makes the heart sick, but desire fulfilled is a tree of life." - Proverbs 13:12 (NIV) (A sick heart can lead to a cold heart if we aren't careful to lean on the Lord.)

"The Lord is near to the brokenhearted and saves the crushed in spirit." - Psalms 34:18 (ESV)

Vision of Marriage Question

What is your understanding of marriage, both practically and spiritually?

Many people go into marriage simply to see what they can get. It isn't always looked at as a place that requires as much giving as receiving. Hopefully, this question reveals a person's vision or expectation for marriage. It will allow you to determine if their thinking is realistic or not and to know if you are on the same page.

Most men know they are the head, but do they actually know what it means and how to walk that out? Most women have heard of submission, but do they know that both the husband and wife have to submit to one another, and that her opinion should be valued enough to be heard and considered, even if the husband decides on a different direction? It's an issue of mutual respect, which has to be in every relationship to make it strong. You should know your outlook on marriage in the following aspects:

A Practical Example of Mutual Respect:

Let's say a husband runs into an old female friend from college. She sends him a friend request on Facebook, but not his wife. She then seeks to be in his life, calling and texting regularly, still not including the wife. In turn, the wife starts feeling uncomfortable because the friend is taking time away from her husband, not involving her at all. The wife ultimately confronts her husband, who can respond in one of two ways: He can show her mutual respect, meaning that he gives her the same consideration he wants from her. Or, he can respond in a way that indicates only his wants and needs matter.

Lack of Mutual Respect Response:

He accuses his wife of being insecure and jealous saying she should just trust him. He continues with his friendship without setting boundaries. When his wife brings it up again, he curses and gets upset; even threatening to leave. This is a man considering only his feelings and not his wife's. His actions show he's selfish and has an imbalanced view of respect in a marriage.

The man isn't the only one who should be respected. The woman's feelings, thoughts, and considerations should be respected as well. Single ladies, if you're dealing with a man who doesn't take the time to communicate and listen when it comes to what's important to you yet shuts down at any sign of accountability, those are red flags. Any man who really wants to be with you will want to talk with you, especially when you're being vulnerable about something that's important to you. That type of vulnerability increases intimacy and will be seen as a plus, instead of a negative, by a man who genuinely values you.

Mutual Respect Response:

He considers his wife's feelings, agreeing to set boundaries that she feels comfortable with. He simply asks her what would make her feel more at ease. The two agree to only receive group texts from the old friend together instead of isolated texts between just her and him. They settle on talking on the phone with the friend when they're all present and create a mutual Facebook account to be used for friends of the opposite sex. This way, both spouses have the account information. Additionally, the husband deletes the request from the old friend and instead adds her to their shared profile.

Marriage:

The Biblically Sound Vision

Man's Role:

Husband is the head, meaning he is the final authority in his household, aside from God. Because of the responsibility he carries, he'll have to walk in humility and submission to Christ in order to lead as Christ.

Scripturally speaking, the husband is a metaphor of Christ and his wife is a metaphor of the church. If a man is pursuing a woman of God who is submitted to Christ, he needs to know she has standards that she didn't make up, but they came specifically from the Word of God.

The man needs to be walking in line with the Word of God to properly lead his household. He must become one who serves and leads as the Bible says the greatest among us are the servants. Because the husband has the greatest responsibility in the home, he'll have to lead by example, serving his household. Jesus himself, as God in the flesh, said that he came not to be served, but to serve. His service to us was an invitation into his world.

> "Not so with you. Instead, whoever wants to become great among you must be your servant, and whoever wants to be first must be your slave--just as the Son of Man did not come to be served, but to serve, and to give his life as a ransom for many." - Matthew 20:26-28 (NIV)

The man sets the standard for his household to follow. If he sets the example that his household should walk in love, his family should follow suit. The man is the protector of his household, physically, emotionally, spiritually, and mentally, and a provider. He is to provide guidance and direction, operating as a source of covering for his family in the ways mentioned above.

Spiritually

Spiritual examples of the man setting the standard could be:

- Studying and teaching the Word of God to his family and praying with them. The giving of tithes and offering.
- Having a genuine relationship with the Lord and allowing his household to see that.
- Not portraying a religious relationship that's domineering, controlling, and based only on works.

A religious relationship is based solely on works and fear. Those who lead this way operate like a tyrant instead of out of a loving and intimate place with the Lord. God is love, so when a man models a relationship with Christ, he should demonstrate genuine love. This means he doesn't love just to get in return, but because of his character. Men have great responsibility in following in the footsteps of Christ.

Practically

A man won't always feel like walking out his role and will sometimes make mistakes. That's fine, but there should be consistent effort and growth in the above-mentioned areas.

Practically, the man is to be the provider for his household. Men represent stability in a sense, providing the foundation for the atmosphere in the home. For example, they have the authority to say peace will rule my home. The way God made their voices deep and straightforward reminds me of the power he has. When the man speaks and says it's going to be okay, it will, indeed, be okay. A woman finds rest in the fellowship of a man who knows who he is and walks in it. This type of man has no need to belittle his woman. Instead, he pushes her to be her best because he knows that she makes him look good. When she flourishes, he flourishes. In many ways, the woman is an extension of her man, which is why women and men must choose wisely by selecting a person who complements them. As women, choosing the wrong man can throw off our ability to be ourselves.

Practically, if a man is only preparing to receive in the relationship and not give, he has ruined his marriage already. A man is responsible for creating a safe environment for his wife to grow and develop. Jesus washes his wife with the water of the word and presents her back to himself (Ephesians 5:25-29).

Many men neglect to set an atmosphere of security and peace for their brides just by simply loving them. Many women, in turn resent, their men and shut down not responding when he operates out of selfish totalitarianism instead of simply loving his lady.

A practical example of this can be easily seen in a dating relationship when the couple agrees to abstain from sex until marriage. The man who changes his mind and punishes his girlfriend or fiancé for wanting to stay true to her commitment to wait is a controlling leader. He no longer respects what she or God wants. Instead, he punishes her for not fulfilling his selfish needs. If a man doesn't value his lady's opinion in dating or courtship, he likely won't change in marriage.

Woman's Role:

A woman is the responder to a man. She's a multiplier and a builder. She's like the electrical outlet that creates light when a man plugs into her. She was made to assist with whatever vision the family has agreed to. If a man wants a peaceful home, she creatively makes it peaceful. If a man sets the tone for a home full of turmoil, he just may get that. Therefore, men have to be very careful about the standard they set in their homes. A woman who's hidden in God before she joins herself with a man should have learned to follow and walk with a man by following and walking with God. However, it's extremely important that women choose wisely because a man can change her nature if she doesn't choose wisely and vice versa. Look at the story of Ahab and Jezebel in the Bible; they had to adapt to each other in order to stay together. If a woman chooses the wrong man, she may find herself changing in ways she doesn't like to make it work. When we aren't allowed to be ourselves in the relationships we've chosen, we end up resenting the relationship and our spouses.

Spiritually

The man, woman, and children should be on one accord under Christ. The man needs to set the standard on the Word of God, prayer, and intimacy with God through love in the home. The woman should reinforce this with the children and within herself. Together, the family should be growing stronger, and the husband and wife should be sharpening one another. It's not that the man is the only one bringing valuable spiritual content to the table; he's listening to his wife and accepting her wisdom also. He just isn't taking a passive role when it comes to being accountable to God through Christ in leading his family.

The woman assists the husband in covering the family in prayer, wisdom, and understanding.

Practically

It can be easy to take for granted when a man is serving and loving us unconditionally. The woman must not do this but continue respecting and honoring him. Even when a woman sees her husband's weaknesses and vulnerabilities, she is to protect them; and the husband is to do the same with his wife. This provides a solid working basis for the machine of the husband and wife team.

She should be careful how she speaks to him by conversing in a manner that builds him up. Wise women build their home, and they build their men. The woman also needs to serve her husband and family in response to her husband's love for her. It's her reasonable service, just like it's the body of Christ's reasonable service to respond as a living sacrifice to Christ.

"And so, dear brothers and sisters, I plead with you to give your bodies to God because of all he has done for you. Let them be a living and holy sacrifice--the kind he will find acceptable. This is truly the way to worship him." - Romans 12:1 (NLT)

Together, the man and the woman figure out how they'll get their household to work for them within the framework of God's word. The woman's service to the husband and household may look like her cooking, cleaning, or it may look like her working outside the home assisting in providing as well.

Domestic roles may vary, depending on the household. For example, there are some men with felony convictions who may have difficulty providing in the form of bringing in lots of income. The woman may work, and the man takes care of home while working as an entrepreneur or in a job that doesn't pay as much. I've also heard of cases where the man became sick and unable to work, so the wife had to go to work to support the family. No situation is the same, but as long as the basic and foundational principles of God's word are followed from that intimate place of revelation and fellowship with Him, the household will be okay.

Side-note: God not only gives us wisdom and revelation regarding spiritual things; He is involved in every area of our lives. When we learn to acknowledge Him in all of our ways, we'll see His wisdom in all areas of our lives.

Collective Role:

Collectively, the husband and wife are a picture of Christ and the church. The major role of marriage here on earth is to reflect the example of Christ's love to His bride, the church. This is a great mystery and something so deep, that it's constantly being revealed throughout the marriage—just as Christ's love for us is consistently shown throughout the entirety of our walk with him. God's love toward us is immeasurably great.

If the relationship isn't reflecting Christ and the church, why isn't it, and what *is* it reflecting? The couple will need to sit down and discuss to determine why.

Is the man using the woman to glaze over his insecurities and to affirm his manhood? Instead, his identity of manhood should be confirmed in Christ.

Unfortunately, too many broken men use women to cover up and gloss over their insecurities. The broken man feels that if he can control a woman—keeping her in check, so to speak—he has successfully accomplished being a man. This notion may be held so that a man can present an image of control to his friends and family. Sorry (not sorry) to burst the broken man's bubble, but being able to control a woman doesn't affirm any man's manhood. This is a lie, and a very costly one at that.

In his single season, a man should have already concluded that he's a man, whether he has a woman in his life or not. A man doesn't become a man by controlling a woman. A man's manhood was determined by God when He assigned the man the appropriate chromosomes in the womb. However, maturity in manhood is something that a man must grow into. He genuinely shows his readiness to be respected as a man by his willingness to take on his God-ordained responsibility.

A man who loves his wife is a man who's worthy of being respected as a man. It takes responsibility to genuinely love a woman, especially to love her like Christ does. This trait should be learned by example from other mature men.

A man cannot simply pursue a woman to be the answer to his selfish need. He has to take on the responsibility of having her in his life. In the Bible, Amnon was sick for the woman he wanted. It was almost like he felt that having the woman he wanted was supposed to make him better, or at least make him feel better. However, he felt worse after he had her. Why?

Because being able to capture a woman physically isn't enough. Tamar, the woman he wanted, stuck around. Why?

Because she expected more. Women require more than being used for selfish purposes by men. They expect men who are willing to rise to the occasion of loving them and protecting their hearts. (See 2 Samuel 13 for story on Tamar & Amnon).

Is the marriage not reflecting Christ because the woman isn't honoring her husband? It is readily acceptable for women to disrespect men in some spaces. We tend to judge men harshly without looking at ourselves as women. There's no disclaimer on the wife honoring her husband. The Bible doesn't say that a woman should honor her husband only if he does everything right or never makes a mistake. It tells us to simply honor our husbands. A woman choosing to honor her husband, even when he falls short, is how she covers her man. She still looks up to him with respect for the simple fact of who he is—her husband. Men need to be valued as much as women do, and it's through respect and honor that they get their sense of value.

Side note: Honoring our husbands does not warrant abuse. Seek the advice of a certified Christian counselor in an abusive situation.

It's so important for women not to nag their men, even when they're right about something. Simply say what needs to be said at an appropriate and well thought out time where you aren't angry, so he can hear your feelings without distraction. If, after you've done this and he still doesn't receive it, he'll have to get it from his superior—Jesus Christ (1 Corinthians 11:3).

I don't know how many times I've spoken to my dad or my brothers about things, and they just wouldn't hear me. So, I said okay and simply took it to my prayer closet. Afterward, God would deal with them, and it would often be a humbling circumstance that forced them to submit to God's word.

When this happens, it's especially important for the woman to have humility and be respectful because God is vindicating her and humbling the man to bring him up to the standard of the Word that He may have spoken through the woman which wasn't accepted, for whatever reason. This doesn't warrant disrespect. If a woman feels like it's gotta get to a point of disrespecting her man, she may need to step away from the situation. Men should, likewise respect and listen to their wives (1 Peter 3:7).

Also, similar to men who look for the woman to validate their manhood, there are women who look to men for validation of their value and worth. These issues must be resolved before marriage or else they could lead a person to choose a partner who isn't good for him/her, causing the marriage to begin at a disadvantage. Resolve to be whole in Christ and to seek a relationship that honors Him prior to marriage.

Finally, both the husband and the wife have to die to themselves and their own selfish motives for the good of the marriage. This is what it means to submit to one another.

> Ephesians 5:21 - submitting to one another in the fear of God. (KJV)

> 1 Corinthians 11:3 - But I want you to realize that the head of every man is Christ, and the head of the woman is man, and the head of Christ is God. (NIV)

When There Is an Unequally Yoked Marriage, It Will Be Harder:

The Unequally Yoked Marriage:

This can be one of the harder ways to reflect God's love. More-than-normal forgiveness is required in this relationship simply because one party lacks the understanding that the believer has and thus, more grace is required.

One prominent example of this in God's word is the story of Hosea and Gomer. Gomer was a prostitute who consistently cheated on Hosea, but God told Hosea to marry her. I believe God commanded this as an example of his great love for us and how we often treat Him yet he still pursues and loves us calling us to repentance. However, outside of this metaphor, I don't believe God wants this to be the norm. As a matter of fact, His word warns against it in the New Testament. Still, many make the choice to be unequally yoked.

To be yoked means to be tied to someone; Therefore, when two people are tied together and going in opposite directions, immediate friction and frustration occurs. This will be so difficult, that the two may find it nearly impossible. The Bible does say that if the unbelieving spouse desires to dwell with the believing spouse after marriage has already taken place, they should not break up. The believing will sanctify the unbelieving spouse. I'm not exactly sure that I have a complete understanding of this, but I'll take a stab at it:

I believe it means that the believing spouse becomes the intercessor for the family. He or she walks in love to the point that the other person becomes convicted and grows in the grace and faith of Christ. Sanctified means being set apart; therefore, the nature of the unbelieving spouse will begin to change, and he or she will become sanctified, cleansed, and set apart. This may take years, however, of persistence, pain, and forgiveness by the believing spouse. Thus, this type of marriage is often so draining, there may be little energy left to devote toward other things. The children will also see this example and begin believing in Christ as well.

> "For the unbelieving husband has been sanctified through his wife, and the unbelieving wife has been sanctified through her believing husband. Otherwise your children would be unclean, but as it is, they are holy." - 1 Corinthians 7:14

Some people were married while both spouses were unsaved, then one party got saved, and the above process began. Others simply went against God's word and became unequally yoked. Those who disobey may have to sacrifice their goals, purposes, and dreams to intercede for their families because their spouses are going in the opposite direction; yet, they are continuously trying to make it work, which is pretty much an impossible task. Doing so will require a lot of dying to self, which is why it's so important to have a marriage that's equally yoked, where both parties are in Christ and at comparable maturity levels, purposes, and plans for one another's lives.

The Equally Yoked Marriage:

This is the easier path because the two parties are going in the same direction. Thus, staying together requires less of a death. However, there will still be give and take, and there will still be dying to self, and forgiving over and over again. It's just easier to stay committed in this scenario since the two have the same goals and vision. This will help the couple push through during the hard times life will throw their way. They can plan and strategize to make their lives easier since they're on one accord.

CHAPTER 5

Part II Answers to Questions Cont'd

What would you say you believe God is doing in your life right now?

Your ability to answer this question, as well as your potential's ability, shows the level of intimacy with God. Is he/she a person who goes with the wind of what everyone else is saying, or can he or she hear God for him/her self? It's very important to be able to hear God for yourself if you are a man who'll lead your home, or if you're a woman who'll assist your husband in leading the home.

Men shouldn't control your life as far as where you'll go and so forth. God should control the reins of your life, and men should affirm, and re-affirm, the instruction God gives you. Repeatedly in scripture, God deals with a man and uses other men to affirm and re-affirm what He says. When God dealt with Saul, blinding him and changing him to Paul, He used a man, Ananias, to affirm what he was doing in Saul and to lay hands on his eyes. When God spoke to Peter regarding salvation being for the Gentiles as well as the Jews, He had already dealt with Cornelius, a Gentile man who feared God. We must be able to hear God to the point where we aren't moved to follow the opinions of men. You may not hear God like other people or as often, but you should have a general idea of how God is leading you in your life. If you feel you're not hearing from God, you may need to go deeper in the Lord instead of pursuing a relationship.

> "Then we will no longer be infants, tossed back and forth by the waves, and blown here and there by every wind of teaching and by the cunning and craftiness of people in their deceitful scheming." - Ephesians 4:14 (Read 4:11-13)

The above-mentioned scriptures speak on God's five-fold ministry in the body of Christ and how it assists us in coming to a place of maturity where we are so firm in who we are in Christ, we aren't tossed to and fro with the next big thing. We ought to be sound enough in our intimate relationship with God to discern what's from him and what isn't. Additionally, a potential should be in tune with the Lord and what he is doing in their life. If they aren't, why not? Are they willing to work on it? Do they even value seeking and hearing God's voice? If this is important to you, it should also be important to your spouse. You don't want someone who demeans or stands in the way of you seeking the Lord. Note that this doesn't mean we'll know everything. This walk with God is a faith-walk, and we learn a lot along the way. A person should have an idea of what God is doing or at least the last thing God confirmed He was doing in their life. This will allow you to see if he/she has learned to walk with God yet.

What are some practices you have to maintain discipline in various areas of your life, such as sexuality, eating habits, spending your time, and money management?

This is more of a personal question; therefore, something less evasive can be asked to determine if he/she has limits or cares enough about his/her purity to set boundaries to protect his/her intimacy with God. Sexual sin is a direct barrier to intimacy with God because it produces condemnation, which is not from God. It's a result of sin and not choosing to obey Him. See "The Single Christian Woman's Guide," and read the chapter called "All About the Hormones." A person willing to set boundaries when it comes to preventing sexual sin is probably serious about his/her purity. Unfortunately, talk is cheap, and when it comes to purity, some guys and girls just talk about it to gain affection from those who are walking their talk. I've had a few guys tell me they'd been abstinent/celibate for three years and wanted to continue down that path, but when it came to putting those words into action, it was a fail, which reminds me, when checking out a potential boo, don't just judge by what he/she says; judge by what he/she does. If a guy says, "I believe in practicing abstinence until marriage," feel free to ask him why it's important to him and how he remains successful at doing so? Ask him if he's willing to implement boundaries into your relationship if you decide to move forward as a couple. That can be an easy way to find out if, indeed, he has boundaries and has established habits for maintaining purity. Someone who is unwilling to set boundaries and/or doesn't stick to theirs are showing red flags. A person should already be living this lifestyle before meeting someone. A man or woman shouldn't pretend in order to earn our affection. That can only last for so long.

A person who buys whatever they want and eats whatever they want with no discipline, is also displaying a red flag. Discipline is a necessary element in self-care and protecting what is valuable. Our minds, bodies, emotions, and relationship with God must be protected as they all reflect our value in some way. If you're a person who has great self-control, you'll have to consider how and if this can work for someone who lacks self-control.

How open are you to correction, and how do you view it? Do you see it as something that can help you grow, or as a put-down to who you are?

This question will assess a person's maturity level as it relates to how willing he/she is to grow and be teachable. These traits are a large part of a successful marriage. It's very important to have someone humble enough for correction because it produces growth as well as well-rounded, well-tempered, and mature people. It also shows the person being corrected that they're genuinely loved.

A person developed in this area will recognize that correction is real love and humble him/herself to receive it. You want a person who knows how and when to humble his/herself. This is a person who's willing to work at what he/she sees as valuable, including a possible marriage with you. Those who refuse correction are often ruled by a spirit of rejection and sometimes rebellion. This causes people to act outside of good character to remedy their rejection.

The only real remedy for rejection is realizing the truth that we're fully loved and accepted in Christ. Thus, we can't work for it, and if we can't work for it, we can't disqualify ourselves from that love. See Ephesians 1:5-7. We should want a person who's willing to accept real love instead of settling for the imitation. Look at Cain, who felt rejected by God because He corrected him concerning his offering. However, instead of him receiving the correction, he rebelled against God, turning against his own brother due to the brokenness of rejection. He didn't see that he'd already been accepted as a son by God. His perspective was so skewed that he saw his brother as the problem, which caused him to feel unloved and unaccepted, when the problem was actually his misguided perspective.

See God's attempt at correction prior to Cain murdering his brother:

"If you do what is right, will you not be accepted? But if you refuse to do what is right, sin is crouching at your door; you are its object of desire, but you must master it." - Genesis 4:7

God shared with Cain why he didn't accept his offering. God accepted him as a son, but not his offering because it wasn't presented correctly. See Genesis 4:1-7

"And have you forgotten the encouraging words God spoke to you as his children? He said, 'My child, don't make light of the LORD's discipline, and don't give up when he corrects you because the Lord disciplines the one he loves, and he chastens everyone he accepts as his son.'" - Hebrews 12:5-6

Thus, correction is not an off-putting of our worth, but an embrace confirming our value and worth. The person who refuses to see correction in this way often ends up in isolation seeking his/her own way. He/she may be very selfish, have a me against the world attitude viewing others as the problem, when he/she's perspective is the actual problem.

Knowing where we stand on all of the questions presented in this book as well as a potential is very important. If we require a particular trait in someone, we should at least have the same standard for our own lives If we don't, our relationships won't have a solid foundation. The questions provide great points for us to consider when thinking about moving forward with a potential partner. They give us a basis for great insight.

I've always said with some people; you don't have to go on a date; you can see what's in their hearts by what comes out of their mouths (See Luke 6:45). And what the mouth doesn't reveal, the actions certainly will. Thus, some potential heartbreaks can be eliminated during the talking phase. You know, those first phone conversations when you're getting to know each other.

Truthfully, I think some of us avoid the talking stage because attractive dates, or dates in general, don't come very often. So, we simply choose to go out. Either way, make sure you're guarding your heart. Be sober. Don't start fantasizing about the relationship being something that it has not yet developed into. Don't allow the fact that you got out of the house on a nice date to blind you to a person's character. Be honest with yourself; if a person isn't for you, they simply aren't for you. Move on. Bow out. Don't stick around just to have someone.

You should be enjoying your life during the interim of singleness anyway. Remember your worth. For my brothers and sisters out there living for God: We are worth it.

CHAPTER 6

Avoid Dating Down

Dating down is when you know a person isn't an appropriate fit for you, yet you date them anyway. I've seen older men and women, who are supposed to know better, do this. Why do we make choices against our better judgement?

> "A person who is full refuses honey, but even bitter food tastes sweet to the hungry." - Proverbs 27:7 (NLT)

The person who is full sees that he has a choice in whether or not to accept what comes along; the person who is hungry will accept anything, whether it's savory or not. Even though he knows his choice may not be good for him, he sees it as a way to satisfy his hunger in the moment.

For that reason, we have to deal with our inner cravings and the voids that often drive us to wrong or codependent relationships. God wants us to depend on him. He's the only one who's always there anyway. He wants us so whole, at peace, and at rest that when it's time to date, we don't even consider entertaining relationships that would be harmful to us.

We have to fill ourselves up on good relationships, friendships, and productive activities. When we are full of good things, we're not desperate to grab onto whatever comes along. Having mature male and female friends, who are walking in the same direction of obedience toward the Lord is an important factor in avoiding desperation.

This will shut down that excessive hunger causing us to be temperate and patient with our romantic needs. Sure, we may not have a spouse yet, but we have safe relationships to share what's on our hearts, reminding us of our worth, and to helping us to grow. If you don't have these things, I'd strongly suggest working on building a healthy community first, instead of dating or looking for a spouse.

The temperance and patience provided in godly community will help you to be balanced and clear on what you want and what you deserve as God's son or daughter. Of course, you can't depend solely on your community; it can't take the place of consistent fellowship with God throughout your day.

Use the space below to make a list of the community you have:
_____
_____
_____
_____
_____
_____
_____
_____

Based on your list, do you feel you have balanced support that helps you stay focused on God's plan for your life as a single believer?

_____
_____
_____
_____
_____
_____
_____

Are you thankful for the community you have?

_____
_____
_____
_____
_____
_____
_____

    When I really thought about it, I realized that I had more community in my life than I thought. I work with a lot of believers who are older women. They love to pour wisdom and support into me, even without me asking. There are various conferences I frequent each year where I've gained support and met new friends who are on the same page as me. God even brought my family closer together. When I stopped to consider this, I realized He's been working on my behalf all along.

At one time, I seemed to lack community among my own peer group. Some of those I'd served with at church had moved on outside of the state, or my friendships seemed to wane becoming more sporadic than consistent as peers got married and had children.

When I noticed this, I became more intentional about placing myself among individuals within my peer group. I prayed to God for wisdom, continued to be myself, and eventually, I found others who valued my presence as much as I valued theirs. It can be a real struggle to find those who love God within your own peer group, but it can be done, and it's needed because it provides a safe place for us to be ourselves. It takes off some of the edge of feeling rejected because of our standard or uniqueness. People date down because they have not fully embraced themselves. We must fully embrace who we are for someone else to appreciate us.

If you feel you don't have enough community what are some practical steps you can take to seek it out?

Some Dating Down Scenarios:

A person who desires to keep you a secret

Ladies, if a man is telling you he's pursuing you and you're the only one who knows it, that's a problem. When a man gets serious about a woman, he'll be glad to let others know that you're his lady. Don't put up with a guy who's been pursuing you but not making it known to friends, family, leaders, or mentors of his and yours.

Situation-ships

When in a relationship, the status should be defined. If you're friends, it should be clear. There should not be any hanky-panky involved in a friendship. The status may be defined as dating/courting, a business relationship, or even friends with benefits. However, as believers, we shouldn't be okay being friends with benefits. We have a higher standard on our lives.

If a man pursues a woman, he should define the relationship and where he wants it to go. Many times, when a man doesn't define the relationship; he is either unsure of what he wants or he is playing games. Someone once said that what doesn't have a definition is left up to personal interpretation. Another person said that indecision is a decision. If we don't want someone playing with our emotions, causing them to go up and down like a roller coaster, then we have to take the responsibility of guarding our hearts. This means being honest and upfront, and sometimes walking away. When dealing with a man who refuses to define the relationship, guarding your heart by walking away or intentionally putting him in the friend-zone are your only options. We don't have time for games out here!

Single Ladies Using Men to Feel Wanted & Vice Versa

Single ladies, we sometimes use guy friends to fill voids that our spouses are supposed to. It's easy for us to form emotional attachments with guy friends and allow conversations to go beyond the line of friendship, including sexual responses and behavior that implies we want something more. Again, let's be honest, stop that, and level up. If we keep playing around with what we don't really want; we may just end up with it. Our male friends aren't to be place holders for our future husbands. We are to trust in God as single women allowing him to fill every space of insecurity. This also applies to single men.

I struggled with similar things when I was in my twenties. I dealt with issues of not feeling loved or wanted.

There were times, I just wanted someone to want me. There were also times I felt I had to reward someone with sex for wanting me. Both men and women use sex to medicate their inner brokenness. It becomes the bandage that never deals with the real root of the problem. And while I'm still a virgin, I'm keeping it real so hopefully, someone can get free. My thoughts were a result of bondage, lust, and confusion. But thanks, be unto God, who dealt with the voids, rejection, and brokenness in me that would have had me making the wrong choices.

This is why it is so important for us to get free instead of jumping in and out of relationships. In becoming free, we should notice a greater depth of who we are and appreciate that. Further, when we date, we will not be willing to compromise who we are just to be in a relationship. In my first book, "The Single Christian Woman's Guide," I discuss knowing our identity and provided space for us to write down some things about it. However, as believers, we aren't to stay in the same place; we're to keep growing into greater depths of who God has called us to be.

In the space below, write out anything new you've learned about yourself. I believe that as God takes us higher in Him, we become more aware of who we truly are. Your answers will create your personal profile of what makes you, you.

Personal Profile:

What Makes You, You?
*Note: You don't have to show anyone this. This exercise is so you are well aware of who you are.

Here's an example.

Spiritually

I'm a teacher with compassion and faith. I can see the good in pretty much any situation. I often see things from a unique perspective that isn't popular, which leaves me feeling isolated at times. This is useful to me as a non-judgmental intercessor. It helps me to pray God's heart for others without personal criticism. When I view people through compassion and grace; its also because I realize that I need God's grace and compassion for my weaknesses as well. I must be careful not to allow people to change that about me because it's a gift from God. I have come to realize that I wasn't made to fit in with everyone.

Natural or Practical

I am astute, but also have a strong sense of humor that balances my intelligence well. I study often. I can be like a sponge to information, especially if it's good.

I love good conversations, learning new things and trying new things because I'm adventurous. I've noted how many teachers are prone to pride; therefore, I discipline myself to be humble and listen to others' opinions to avoid pride.

Outlook on Life

My current view is to trust God and take risks, walking by faith in areas that perhaps I was afraid to before. Either way, I trust that God's got me.

Complete a Brief Personal Profile for Yourself Below:

Spiritual Characteristics About Me:
_____
_____
_____
_____
_____

Natural or Practical Things About Me:
_____
_____
_____
_____
_____

My Current Outlook on Life:
_____
_____
_____
_____
_____

When you have someone who complements you, there's a better chance at staying together since he or she will allow you to be yourself in the relationship. The only change you should make is growing and maturing into a better you. When you feel you have to discard what makes you, you, you're dating down. Dating on your level or dating up not only allows the other person to improve, it also sharpens you. Both parties sharpen one another in a healthy relationship. It should not simply be one-sided.

Relationships sent by God should refine you.

> "As iron sharpens iron, so a friend sharpens a friend." - Proverbs 27:7

A friend has the best interest of his friend at heart. He isn't trying to use his friend for selfish purposes and then on to the next one. Make sure you protect your heart as you discern the purpose of a potential in your life. What are they here for? What is it that they are looking for? What is it that you are looking for? If the purpose does not align with what God has for you, are you willing to let it go and wait on God's best?

CHAPTER 7

Case Studies

Scripturally speaking, there is a time and a place for every purpose under the sun. When it's time to date, we should be prepared. "Studies have repeatedly found that couples who are similar in areas such as socioeconomic status, education, age, ethnicity, religion, attractiveness, attitudes, values, and intelligence are more likely to be satisfied with their relationships and are less likely to seek divorce." (*The Defining Decade*, Jay).

In her book, "The Defining Decade," Meg Jay shares that the more similarities couples have, the less likely they'll be to seek divorce and the happier they will be. This is also indicated as truth by scripture when we look at the virtuous woman, who had to meet her match in her husband to acquire marriage.

We generally focus on the woman in Proverbs 31, but it also hints at an incredible man who was her counterpart. It begins by talking about a man who knows he's a king because he was taught to be one by his mother. She also taught him not to be loose with women, to be careful where he invested his money, and to remain sober, avoiding becoming drunk with alcohol.

> "Do not spend your strength on
> women, your vigor on those who ruin
> kings. It is not for kings, Lemuel—
> it is not for kings to drink wine,
> not for rulers to crave beer,
> lest they drink and for-
> get what has been decreed,
> and deprive all the oppressed of their rights.
> Let beer be for those who are perishing,
> wine for those who are in anguish!
> Let them drink and forget their poverty
> and remember their misery no more.
> Speak up for those who can-
> not speak for themselves,
> for the rights of all who are destitute.
> Speak up and judge fairly;
> defend the rights of the poor and
> needy." Proverbs 31:3-9 (NIV)

I believe his strength and vigor in verse three represented his income, which is what men are paid for utilizing their strength and skills on the job. Many men get caught up paying child support to a woman they didn't intend to be with because they gave their strength to her. However, the men who know they are kings avoid this. They practice sobriety in their decisions and good judgment, while also standing up for those less fortunate than themselves.

Later the scripture talks about how the virtuous woman's husband is known at the city gates, which means he has a reputation of nobility and integrity. In ancient times, this place was a significant aspect of the city's business hub. Judicial proceedings took place at the city gates, elders sat there judging matters, and kings addressed their citizens at the city gates.

The virtuous woman wasn't alone in being a well-rounded individual of noble character; her husband was also. This speaks to the idea that we attract who we are. While I believe that statement is true to a large extent, it's not in all cases. We can't be responsible for everyone who's attracted to us, but we can be accountable for who we give a chance to. If a person isn't complementing who we are, they don't deserve an opportunity to be with us.

Some people will have nearly everyone attracted to them because they're just that magnetic, but not everyone will meet their standard. Just like bugs are attracted to the light when it's dark, some people stand out so much, they attract all kinds. This is why your discernment must be on key.

I'm not saying your spouse needs to be superman or superwoman, but you should accept someone who complements who you are instead of taking away from it. Couples who are similar in important foundational things, such as values, are the ones with the highest chance of remaining together.

When choosing someone to spend the rest of your life with, you want to choose someone who aligns with who we are, our value system, purpose, and goals. Things like socioeconomic status can change. God promises men favor who take a wife anyway. Thus, often a man's income will increase once married. I've seen this on more than one occasion. It's more important to have a man who is diligent and has a demonstrated hard-work ethic; than to have a man with a whole lot of money. The Bible promises that the diligent will not lack.

Below are examples that will allow you to practice discernment in a dating/courtship scenario. While reading them, think about each person's personal value system and note if they're choosing a partner based on what's important to them or if they're short-changing themselves. Also, determine if they should continue with the relationship or let it go.

Case Study # 1 - Tavia & Terrell

Tavia met Terrell, who asked her out. Both were Christians and went to church, and the two dated over a period of time. They both voiced that getting married was the purpose for them seeing each other. Additionally, they agreed to wait until marriage to have sex. Terrell seemed very sweet, opening doors, picking her up from her house, and making sure she made it home safely. After dating for a couple of months, the two decided to commit to courtship.

Tavia wanted to set boundaries for their relationship, but Terrell didn't see the need because he said he was disciplined. However, Tavia set boundaries for herself and voiced them to Terrell, one being she didn't want to get physical prematurely and to avoid doing so, she did not do Netflix and chill. She'd be behind closed doors with him in his place when someone else was in his home and vice versa with her own house.

Terrell, on the other hand, did want to get physical after agreeing to a courtship. However, he only wanted to be affectionate behind closed doors, he said to Tavia, when she questioned him about why he was not affectionate with her. She'd often wondered why Terrell wasn't affectionate while they were out together. He wouldn't hold her hand unless she asked him to. When they were at the movies; he wouldn't place his arm around her, even when Tavia tried to suggest it in a classy way.

He told her that he would be patient with her in her not wanting to kiss right away, and he seemed to be. Terrell appeared to be working for Tavia's affection. He sacrificed some of his time to be with her and made her feel special. He paid for everything, never cursed at her, always opened the door, and would spend time with her even when he had important things to do.

Tavia saw him as sweet and somewhat humble—something she'd never experienced before. She was impressed to a degree but desired more of an intimate connection emotionally, spiritually, and mentally before kissing Terrell. In preparation for his physical reward, Terrell would seek to make Tavia comfortable by reassuring her that if anything made her uncomfortable, once they began being physical, he would stop.

Tavia never thought much of it. One day, Terrell invited her to his home. She said she'd go but reminded Terrell of her personal boundary of not going to her boyfriend's house unless someone else would be there. She asked if someone else would be there, to which he responded that he didn't know. She said she'd call before heading out, just to make sure.

Tavia called Terrell a couple of hours later, but he didn't respond. She stayed home, watching TV, yet he still didn't return her call. Turns out, Terrell was upset. He gave her the silent treatment for some time after that. When they finally talked again, he shared that they could no longer be together because he felt she didn't trust him. Terrell also mentioned that he resented Tavia asking him to attend a double date at her house, where she would've cooked dinner and discussed an online event they were to watch with her best friend and her best friend's husband. She was also upset that she and Terrell didn't connect more. Resenting her idea of accountability, he told her he didn't need a babysitter. During one of their final conversations, Tavia asked Terrell why he couldn't just love her. He responded that he didn't know her well enough to love her. He also told her about several situations when he'd been with other women with whom he'd practiced abstinence and how they'd spent the night at each other's houses, holding each other, watching TV, and sleeping in each other's arms, and nothing happened.

The two separated and tried being friends until Terrell found another woman who was okay with sex before marriage. He proposed to her, while Tavia moved on.

Examine the Above Case Study:

What do you think Terrell's Personal Profile was? What were some things he valued personally?

_____
_____
_____

Spiritually?

_____
_____
_____

Natural or Practically?

_____
_____
_____

What was his outlook on life?

_____
_____
_____

Were they a good match? Why or why not?

_____
_____
_____

My Take on Terrell's Personal Value System

Spiritually

Terrell seemed to be carnal and headstrong. His needs were placed before a need to please God. Thus, he was religious only having a form of godliness, yet denying God's full power to keep him as a single man of God.

He was manipulative and unwilling to yield completely to the Lord. He should have been the one protecting the relationship but left it up to Tavia. Then, he punished her for not submitting to his ill leadership. In his religious perspective, he does things based on works, expecting a reward; however, he's unwilling to sacrifice and hang in there when it seems the pay-off isn't immediate.

Naturally or Practically

Terrell appears to value hard work:

Culturally, he did everything acceptable for a man to do while courting a woman. But Biblically speaking, as a man of God, he didn't. Terrell viewed his actions toward Tavia as work that would be rewarded with another of his values: physical connection. He expected Tavia to compromise values to be with him; he felt he deserved it because he had "worked" for it.

Terrell seemed to place a high value on physical connection:

It wasn't that he was against connecting with Tavia. He just wanted to express it in a physical manner behind closed doors and prioritized this over an emotional, mental, and spiritual connection.

The Bible says a 3-fold cord is not easily broken. The relationships of those who rely too heavily on being physical can be compared to a fire that needs to be kept burning. A relationship based solely on physical intimacy will need it consistently to survive. When the couple becomes tired of just sex, the relationship falls apart. It cannot last because focusing most of your energy on a physical connection isn't enough to keep a relationship going for years. If Tavia had fallen for this, she'd likely be in a loveless relationship with a man who didn't care enough to love her but sought to use her.

Terrell's Outlook on Life

Terrell was self-seeking, and it was all about the now to him. What did he want in the moment? The good things he did for Tavia were done with a selfish motive. Had he done things genuinely, because he loved her, he would've been consistent with his actions. The Bible is clear: Love is not self-seeking. Love endures all. Love protects, always trusts, always hopes, always perseveres.

Tavia wasn't protected mentally or spiritually walking with Terrell, and she would only be protected physically when walking in agreement with him. When Terrell didn't get what he was looking for, he was gone.

What do you think Tavia's Personal Profile was? What were some things she valued personally?
___
___
___

Spiritually?
___
___

Naturally or Practically?
___
___

What was her outlook on life?
___
___

Were they a good match? Why or Why not?
___
___

My Take is Below:

Spiritually

Tavia valued being obedient to the Lord, despite the discomfort in having to let Terrell go.

She was willing to be uncomfortable for a period of time and wait for a better future with someone who shared her values. Tavia practiced discipline and went without her heart's desire for a time to be obedient to God.

Naturally or Practically

Tavia Valued Love

She continued with Terrell, in hopes he would give her something he wasn't genuinely equipped to: love. Tavia kept the relationship going, wishing that Terrell would change or grow. On some level, she didn't love herself enough, so she stuck around for a man who didn't want to change. Terrell's words did not line up with his actions when it came to celibacy until marriage. Tavia ignored this in hopes of being loved by Terrell because he was a good guy and the best she'd ever had to pursue her.

Tavia Valued Emotional, Mental, and Spiritual Connection as a foundation prior to being physical.

It wasn't that she wasn't attracted to Terrell, but she needed more. Tavia understood that when you have a strong foundation, the relationship will be more solid and that the physical stuff would happen when it was appropriate. She also knew that being physical too soon could cloud good judgement making her think she had a greater investment than she actually had in the relationship.

Tavia set boundaries to avoid giving into her weak flesh. However, the fact that she was the only one to do so should have shown her that she and Terrell weren't on the same page.

Tavia valued communication and having someone in her corner.

She wasn't used to having someone who was down for her. So, when Terrell initially pursued her quite seriously, Tavia overlooked everything because she wasn't used to having someone by her side, and it was something she'd desired. Sometimes, we allow things to continue longer than they should because it's filling a void in us, but not in the way God ordained.

Tavia's Outlook on life:

She seems to have faith that one day, her desire for a godly marriage would be fulfilled. Therefore, she wasn't willing to settle for anything less than a godly relationship. She's well on her way.

Summary:

The situation was a good experience. Both parties had good qualities, but the couple was not a good fit for each other. While they stated they had the same goals initially, as time went on, it was clear that that they each had very different purposes for the relationship. The man didn't take the lead spiritually in a manner that honored God. This left the woman to lead herself, which fostered division at the beginning of the relationship. This was a big sign for Tavia.

Additionally, Terrell was actually being low-key manipulative by refusing to speak to her after she wouldn't do what he wanted. A person often manipulates to produce their will with another person's life instead of God's will. It appears that Terrell didn't have an intimate relationship with God because he related primarily off of the idea of payment for work when it came to his relationship with Tavia. He lacked an understanding of God's grace and real love. Without a proper understanding of those aspects, he couldn't love himself the way he should, and if he couldn't do that, then he definitely wouldn't have been able to love Tavia the way she needed to be loved. It's almost like Terrell was putting on a show for her, hoping to get paid for his entertainment at the end of the night. Unfortunately, all to often, self-love, intimacy with God, and practical matters aren't taught to men as much as they are to women. As a result, many women are used as experiments, while men search for the validation of what it means to be a man in relationships.

Tavia did what she could but ultimately needed to come to the realization that the man she wanted wasn't at the maturity level that she required. She'd been built differently by God, and thus, by dating Terrell, she was dating down. Yes, he was interested in her and was available, but he wasn't on her same level. And had she continued on with him, Tavia would've had to dumb herself down unless he decided to grow, which is something many women do.

She could've very easily settled for a one-sided relationship where she did all of the compromising so they could stay together. However, she would've had to be okay with not being loved and accepted for who she genuinely was. She would have been with a man who only appeared to be what she wanted and needed. When Terrell rejected her for not breaking her boundary, she should've realized he wouldn't be consistent in a relationship. Instead, she tried to work it out, wanting him to just love her. When a woman is secure in her worth, she doesn't beg a man to love her. If he sees her worth, he'll simply do so. If he doesn't, he's not the one for her.

Terrell, and men like him, can find plenty of women on their level, who'd be ecstatic to be with him. He just isn't for a woman like Tavia.

We must realize that just because someone is a good person doesn't mean they're good for us. This is where knowing ourselves comes in. When we know who we are, we have a clear path of where we want to go, and anyone who doesn't want to come along will be left behind. God bless Terrell. He has a different path to walk, and Lord willing, he'll learn all he needs to on that journey.

It's good that Tavia realized the importance of building a healthy, non-sexual relationship first. It's also important to note that it's easier to practice abstinence when both parties are in agreement. Boundaries are important so we can protect whatever we consider valuable, and we are very valuable.

Tavia could have very easily fallen into another trap often laid for women, which is taking on the headship role in a relationship instead of allowing the man to do so. In many cases, if the man isn't acting as the spiritual leader, the woman takes on the responsibility. She feels forced into it since her partner isn't doing it. This can also cause the woman to feel resentful toward the man, which can lead to anger, bitterness, control, division, separation and even end in divorce. That's why it's so important to choose someone who desires the type of marriage you do. Your vision must be clear and should be discussed with a potential before marriage.

At my old church, I attended an awesome marriage prep course. They encouraged us to write a personal vision for our marriages and to construct a mutual vision with our spouses when the time came. This is a valuable activity as it states our expectations upfront instead of leaving the other person guessing, and possibly having to face disappointment in the marriage.

Terrell and Tavia could have worked out if they were on the same page. A relationship won't work if each person has their own separate agenda. To make a relationship work, we have to approach it with an "us" mentality instead of a "me," which is why even though Terrell and Tavia were good people, they weren't good for each other.

Case # 2

Arielle and Thomas

Arielle was one of the last single ones in her group of friends. While her friends were getting married and relocating around the country, she was focused on her purpose. However, one day, she looked up and realized she was getting older and began regretting the fact that she was still single. On top of that, Arielle had been waiting for marriage to have sex. Many of her friends and peers who'd decided not to wait were in committed marriages, causing her to question if the continued wait was truly worth it. So, she decided to try something different.

She began a relationship with Tyler, a pastor at her local church. After he started pressuring Arielle to remove her boundaries, she gave in. She was somewhat broken in her thinking. Arielle felt she'd tried to do things the right way in the past, but things didn't turn out as she expected. About a year and a half into her and Tyler's relationship, Arielle got pregnant. She had a little girl, and not long after, she and Tyler broke up. Ultimately, she decided to relocate to another church to heal from her breakup. During the process, Arielle struggled with the idea of condemnation and whether she'd be good enough for a man of God who genuinely loved her. This is when she met Thomas, who was enamored by her beauty, inside and out.

She shared with Thomas that she wasn't interested in a relationship because she felt she needed to continue healing. He respected her wishes but continued to think about her, and she thought about him from time to time as well. Finally, Thomas gave it another shot, while Arielle struggled with the idea that such a strong man of God would want her. After all, she had a child and struggled with feeling condemned. However, Thomas was so loving toward Arielle, she could not resist. She got caught up in the idea of it all and began dating Thomas.

He accepted her even though she'd had a child out of wedlock. But, because she still struggled with her worth, she found it hard to believe that Thomas truly wanted to be with her. One day, when her child's father dropped their daughter off, she fell weak and slept with him. She hadn't broken that soul-tie and was still looking for validation from her ex.

The guilt she felt was overwhelming, so she shared this information with Thomas. He was hurt, but after a while, he forgave her, and they continued seeing each other. Thomas felt that if he could just love her enough, she'd see it was far better to be with him—a good man of God. The couple eventually got married but went through a separation as Arielle continued to struggle with rejection while constantly trying to push Thomas away by saying hurtful things and comparing him to her ex.

Thomas had anger issues of his own at times. He would lash out because he was frustrated by always being the person in his family to see about everyone. Many times, he sacrificed what was important to him to make sure his family and friends were doing well. All the while, Thomas forgot to treat himself with the same care he gave to others. In a sense, he found his identity in saving and helping others. So, when he realized he couldn't just fix Arielle, he was crushed. It caused him to second guess himself and his worth. After two years of separation and personal self-care, the couple decided to go to counseling, where some of their issues were uncovered. They're still married and have re-adjusted to living together as a couple.

What do you think Arielle's Personal Profile was based on the story? What were some things she valued personally?

Spiritually?

Spiritually, Arielle seemed to start out well but became discouraged after a while. Initially, she appeared to value obeying God but changed in order to be accepted. She knew that she needed God and that she needed to be around believers, so attending church was important to her. She valued her wholeness but struggled to take the necessary steps to get there. Arielle needed to increase her trust in God. Perhaps, God wanted to use the situation of her being the single friend, to press into trusting Him more. Like Arielle, many of us get tripped up when we don't feel our lives line up with what we desire from God. Instead our lives appear to be contradictory to what we've expected. Her obedience didn't seem to pay off, so she tried something different. I feel for Arielle because I've gone through this test personally, and it's very hard.

Naturally or Practically?

Arielle simply wanted to be loved, which was very important to her. She didn't want to feel left behind. She valued fitting in with her friends and peers and being a part of something, even at the expense of her peace.

She became double-minded when she started paying more attention to her circumstances than God's will and purpose for her life. This uncertainty showed in her actions and, ultimately, the consequences.

What was her outlook on life?

In the end, she learned from her experience and grew with her husband. Arielle's perspective was to continue to trust God and grow. Previously, she felt like life hadn't been fair to her. Arielle compared herself to her friends, which is how she fell into the trap of the broken thinking that created broken actions in her life. These broken actions produced a broken cycle of constantly looking for validation in others. She needed to deal with her lack of self-worth which was at the root of her actions.

Below are some characteristics that can be seen in Arielle and Thomas. Do you see any of these traits within yourself? How can you strengthen the good ones and extinguish the bad ones?

Rejection	Low self-worth	Commitment	Forgiveness	Identity in Work
Unbelief	Savior Syndrome	Lack of self-love	Wrong perspective of self	

What do you think Thomas' Personal Profile was based on in the story? What were some things he valued personally?

Spiritually?

He had a relationship with God.

Naturally or Practically?

He seemed to take a backseat to valuing himself. He valued having a wife and Arielle's beauty, but he put up with a lot and was drawn to people who needed help. Thomas found value in assisting others while sacrificing his own wants and needs. Additionally, he needed to work on his wholeness.

What was his outlook on life?

Thomas wanted to be a savior to others, which could have been a pride issue. He was going to make things work, no matter what. God may have wanted Thomas to lean and depend on him more and to become more balanced. Thus, this situation likely worked for his good in that he wasn't in control for some time. This forced him to deal with himself instead of hiding behind helping others. His outlook on life definitely became stronger after facing his own challenges with his personal value and worth after he and Arielle separated.

Summary:

First, I'm glad the couple worked out. They were only able to do so because both parties were willing to be committed. It's difficult when only one party wants to make it work. I briefly wrestled over if the couple should stay together or not, but chose to make the point that couples don't always come together being whole or making all the right decisions. Sometimes, they're a mess when they come together, but God gives grace to those couples when they're willing to receive it. As a teacher, I want to be balanced in sharing that just because people aren't whole when they get married doesn't mean they're condemned to hell. There will, however, be some additional challenges that the couple will have to endure, but with God's grace, a strong commitment, and godly wisdom, anything is possible. Some things, we don't have to go through; we have a choice at avoiding some hardships. The best decision is to marry and date while whole, meaning sober in your thinking and actions. Whole people aren't led by the voids they feel, but by wisdom and God's Spirit.

Let's look at some of the brokenness of Arielle and Thomas before they were married. First, she allowed fear to make her to think she was missing out on something because all her friends were getting married and moving on with life while she was still single. She'd been pursuing purpose and enjoying life until she began feeling something was wrong with her. Her brokenness began showing, producing a mindset tainted by fear. Remember, broken perspectives create broken thinking, which produces broken actions.

This is a trick of the enemy. He'll often make us feel like we're doing something wrong if we aren't getting to a desired place as quickly as our peers. But the devil is a liar! God has a timeline that we must consistently surrender to. The second lie that Arielle believed was that it was her celibacy that was causing her to stay single. She saw that her married friends and peers didn't practice celibacy like she did. This led to her trying something different. She assumed she was rejected because she chose to practice celibacy, so she took things into her own hands. In her mind, she would get a man to accept her by compromising her vow to remain celibate until marriage, which led to further brokenness.

Arielle was operating out of unbelief, disloyalty to God, and idolatry in order to be accepted by men. She was willing to sacrifice everything to be in a relationship—even her own peace of mind.

Arielle didn't fully accept herself because if she had, she wouldn't have compromised to receive false love from Tyler, who took advantage of the situation. She would have guarded her heart, realizing her worth. Because of this, she struggled with soul-ties and condemnation.

Fear was the culprit that led Arielle down the path of wrong thinking and wrong decisions. We have to recognize fear when it comes and build up faith to remove it from our lives. She was doing well before she allowed fear to get the best of her. Many times, we'll be progressing nicely, and the enemy will send something in our lives to distract us and get us off course. The Bible says not to faint in well doing because in due season, we will reap if we faint not. Arielle could have made a different choice that would have saved her from some heartache. Thankfully, things turned out okay with her and Thomas, but she still had to break away from the wrong thoughts that caused her to make unhealthy choices later on in life. Even if we don't deal with our brokenness immediately, we'll have to deal with it at some point. The sooner we deal with it, the better—especially before we invite someone else into the mess our brokenness can and will create if left unchecked. Who knows what God had for Arielle had she stayed on the original course?

Thomas was a good man who went through some crazy stuff with Arielle. He seemed to have a hero mentality, wanting to save her. He found his value and worth in fixing other people's problems while ignoring his own. It's great to help others, but we have to realize we need help, too. No one has it all together. Because Thomas was a fixer, he willfully went into a relationship with a woman who hadn't fully decided that she was rocking with him. He provided what Arielle needed at the time, but her brokenness wouldn't allow her to appreciate it completely.

Thomas continued putting himself at risk, not only taking on Arielle as his girlfriend, but his wife also. Had she decided against making it work, he would've been out on a limb by himself, trying to figure it out. It's best to allow a person to heal and work on themselves prior to marriage. However, if a couple chooses to move forward anyway, they should know it will be a greater battle. Battles are sometimes won, and other times, they are lost, but there's a greater risk of losing when one or both parties are broken.

Case # 3

Christopher and Tavia, Then Charles & Tavia

Christopher and Tavia met in a Facebook group for Christian singles. Tavia thought Christopher was kind of cute, so even though they lived in different states, she added him as a friend. She liked many of his posts and commented here and there because he seemed to be so mature considering his posts. It was obvious he'd been through some things in his life and was dependent on the Word of God for the right perspective on life, and Tavia was often encouraged by his posts. For about a week, Christopher took a break from Facebook.

When he returned, Tavia was so glad to see him that she commented on his status about how she missed him and his encouraging posts. Christopher was flattered and DMed her his number with an invitation for her to call anytime. One day, she took him up on that offer. She started by making small talk with the brotha, asking what he thought about a particular topic. Christopher brushed off her question quickly asking her when she'd be willing to move to his state. Tavia paused for a second, then chuckled because surely, he had to be joking, but Christopher wasn't laughing. He was serious.

Tavia kept his question in the back of her mind as he said he'd call her right back because his daughter was on the other line. He didn't return her call, so she thought it might have been due to the awkwardness of the conversation. Tavia decided to address his question via text, letting Christopher know she wasn't comfortable jumping right into a relationship and that she preferred getting to know him as a friend first and seeing if things went further. He responded by asking her to call him later that night. She texted to let him know that her schedule wouldn't allow her to call for three days, then Tavia ultimately called him back. She left him a voicemail but never got a call back.

Over time, Tavia starts noticing strange posts from Christopher about his baby's mama. It was like he was talking to/about her in his statuses instead of communicating directly to her. Since his daughter was already a teenager, Tavia assumed any baby-mama drama would be resolved.

Several months had gone by when Christopher texted Tavia out of the blue. She started receiving messages, starting with the infamous, "good morning, beautiful," and also "enjoy your day, beautiful," and "God is gonna bless you with favor today my love." Mind you, they hadn't had any other conversations aside from the initial phone call. However, Christopher was acting like they were already in a relationship, even though they hadn't even built a healthy foundation.

Tavia decided to guard her heart. She texted Christopher back, explaining that she would no longer respond to his messages as she felt the texts were ones a man would be sending a potential wife. Christopher was confused because he thought his texts proved he was pursuing Tavia. He tried to explain, but eventually told her that he would respect her wishes.

She continued enjoying life, guarding her heart, and pursuing her purpose. Tavia also decided to volunteer as a panelist with other authors at a local bookstore's event. Also, on the panel was a like-minded man, Charles, who was taken by her thoughtful insight. After the event, the two authors exchanged business cards. He gave her a call the next day, and asked if she wanted to meet for coffee. Tavia agreed, and they ended up talking for three hours.

They found that they complimented each other. They had similar goals, desired marriage, and both were very devoted to God, family, helping people, and themselves. Tavia didn't have to wonder how Charles felt about her. He told her every chance he got, and more importantly, he showed her that he wanted her. Charles never forced her to do anything that went against her beliefs. He respected her and saw her as valuable, so he protected her. He took the lead in setting boundaries for the purpose of honoring God; Tavia didn't even have to bring it up. He had godly men around him who held him accountable in having a clear vision for his life before adding a woman to the equation. Tavia had met her match. When her friends, family, and mentors all met Charles, they fell in love with him as well.

Tavia, who is now engaged, was so glad she waited and chose not to give up or settle for any of the previous guys. Of course, Charles and Tavia have disagreements and will have to grow together, but they are committed to each other and the process of growing together.

Do you think it was good that Tavia passed on Christopher? Why or why not?

_____
_____
_____
_____
_____

Do you think Charles & Tavia should stay together? Why or why not?

_____
_____
_____
_____
_____

Summary:

Christopher obviously had some irrational ideas that he failed to acknowledge and address. He had made irrational decisions twice. Once was when he assumed a woman would pick up and move for a stranger she didn't know without first building up to that. Sensible people generally wouldn't ask something like that during a first conversation.

The second time was when he failed to communicate with Tavia for a while, then started texting her again like they'd been talking the entire time. Part of the issue could have also been that Christopher simply didn't have good communication skills. He may have been well-developed in the religious community, relaying information about scripture, but he might have been inexperienced when it came to relating to people. In fact, many religious people don't understand the value of self-development.

Unfortunately, many are so enamored with the idea of being in a relationship that they fail to realize that their personal development as a single person is as important as their desire for marriage. Healthy and balanced individuals make healthy couples, and that was something Christopher needed to acknowledge. If he never takes his growth and development seriously, he would likely continue to experience the cycles of getting with desperate women, who are willing to accept anything.

Tavia was honest about what she wanted and valued. We learned earlier on, in her relationship with Terrell, that connecting with her spouse mentally, emotionally, and spiritually was important to her. While Christopher offered the spiritual aspect, he lacked maturity mentally and emotionally.

Tavia wanted to honor God, and her now fiancé' wanted the same. She valued discipline and setting boundaries to ensure this, and so did Charles. Additionally, Tavia wanted someone who respected her as much as she respected herself, and Charles was that man.

He's actually a lot like Boaz in the Bible. Boaz demonstrated some of the characteristics mature women of God expect.

He was a provider.

Boaz provided for Ruth, giving her extra grain for herself and her mother-in-law.

He was a protector.

Boaz protected Ruth, making sure she stayed in a safe area while working in his field. He didn't want any harm to befall her, such as rape or sexual harassment.

He did what was necessary to have the woman he desired.

A determined Boaz, quickly, went to the man who was next in line to have Ruth as his wife. Afterward, he went to the city gate, where legal proceedings took place, and filed the necessary paperwork to seal the deal for his spouse. There was no guessing or wondering if he wanted her. Ladies, we are all worth this. And we still must treat ourselves like we're worthy, whether we've experienced someone treating us like this or not. By owning our worth, we'll be ready for a man like this when he crosses our path.

He valued and respected her.

Boaz respected Ruth outside of what she could offer with her body. He wanted to protect her reputation as well. Boaz made sure no one thought she was creeping with the boss man, so he didn't touch her sexually before sealing the deal of marriage. He made this statement regarding Ruth, "No one must know that a woman came to the threshing floor."

These are things Charles offered Tavia. She didn't have to worry about being manipulated, nor did she have to raise him up or pressure him to be responsible. He was already walking in his role, as Tavia likewise walked in hers as a mature, responsible, and honorable woman of God.

Even though she'd experienced disappointment in the past, on more than one occasion, she kept standing on her personal values. It eventually paid off for her. Will you stand on your values like Tavia did, not settling for anyone less than one who complements who you genuinely are? If you're not sure what your values are, you aren't ready to date. If your values have not been tested, they may not be firm enough.

God wants to build us up first, before placing us with another. Sometimes, due to impatience, loneliness, and other reasons, we attempt to make things work that were never intended to. Then, we—or even our children—end up paying for it. Please, take your growth seriously and develop into the best version of you in Christ. Christ has made us whole, free, vision-oriented, and intentional. Don't rush whatever season you're in. Enjoy your life, and your relationship with God being led by wisdom and His Spirit. Take note of what you've learned about yourself and how you relate to others.

What are some of your characteristics? What upsets you? What brings you joy? Consider some of these things when it's time to date. You'll need to choose someone you can live with and who's a great match for you. Making the right decision is more critical than being able to say you're taken or married. Don't settle for someone just because you feel you're running out of time. In fact, more time can be lost if you pick the wrong person. That's time you can never get back.

Remember: God has his best for you. In His word, He's given us the tools to choose wisely. The question is, will we use them?

CHAPTER 8

Nuggets

Love You First:

If you're trying to love a potential mate like 1 Corinthians 13 says without first loving yourself, you're out of order. Read more about this in the book, "The Wholeness Action Plan." Pay special attention to the chapter that asks if you're in a healthy relationship with yourself.

Healthy Boundaries Keep You Safe and They Show You Who is Serious About You:

Anything of high value needs to be protected. That's why there are often security guards where there are large groups of people; people are valuable, and you are too. Having boundaries is a way to communicate your value to others.

An example of a healthy boundary is Tavia not going to her man's house alone to Netflix and chill. If he really liked her, he would've saw the value in her boundary and worked with her to create a solution they were both comfortable with. In a relationship, only healthy compromises should be made; you get something you need, and the other party gets something they need without belittling one another. If you find that you're criticized for having a healthy boundary, the other person doesn't really care about you and may only be looking to use you for their selfish purposes.

Don't be moved by a potential who doesn't see your worth:

It just means this person isn't for you. Be willing to move on and to remain steadfast in how you personally value yourself, in spite of how you're seen. You are still worthy.

Don't diminish who you are to be loved:

If you cannot be yourself, as God made you, around him/her, he/she isn't the one. Be okay with keeping it moving.

It doesn't mean you're a failure if you're single at an older age:

You haven't failed just because you've been single longer than others. This is a lie Satan uses to get us to think of ourselves as less-than so we'll adapt a hopeless mindset that will result in making poor choices. Continue to walk with wisdom and trust in God.

Loving God will get you through a lot of stuff:

The Bible says that if we love God, we'll keep his commandments, which is so true. The more we grow in our love for God, the easier it will be to obey him. Make growing your love for God one of your personal goals, and you'll notice an ease in wanting to obey Him. It doesn't feel like work when it's love. This helps you to endure through the hard places that come with obeying God.

Remember to enjoy life:

Being single should be one of the most exciting times in our lives, due to the freedom to explore, experience, and grow. We should be discovering life, ourselves, the world, and cherishing new encounters that allow us to grow. Don't work so much in your singleness that you forget to actually live life.

All wounds heal in a healthy functioning body:

Even if you don't feel healed, whole, or free now, eventually, you will if you continue behaving in a manner that brings about healing (see "The Wholeness Action Plan" book). Wholeness will be vital in your ability to properly become one with another.

Don't focus too much on being in a relationship:

If you're single and see no potentials, or if you have a crush, don't focus all of your energy on it. Doing so can make you feel uncontent and dissatisfied in the present, robbing you of enjoying your life right now. Being anxious and discontented in singleness, almost always causes bad relationship choices. You want to make relationship decisions from a place of wholeness, peace, faith, and the leading of the Holy Spirit, not anxiety and dissatisfaction.

Remember God is Your Father:

God is covering you and keeping you safe. He also removes people from our lives when they aren't right for us because He loves us. I've experienced God doing this when I lacked the boldness to do it myself. Trust God's leading. The rejection that He permits is for our protection.

Don't force a relationship:

Remember that it's God who puts godly relationships together, not us. If you find yourself forcing a relationship instead of letting God's grace empower it to move forward, you may be setting yourself up for disappointment.

When it comes to love:

Wait for what's right, not for what's available.

On hiding your relationship:

If you feel you have to hide your relationship from godly accountability, it's probably not of God. Be careful not to let pride destroy you.

Single ladies…

If a man only chooses to love you based on what you can give him, he really doesn't love you at all.

Avoid making decisions based on competition or pressure:

Don't allow competition or pressure to drive you into a relationship God didn't ordain. You have nothing to prove, so avoid this trap. You're not in a race to see who can marry first or to prove you're good enough to be in a relationship.

Be aware of a selfish person:

A self-centered individual often enters one-sided relationships, where he/she is being served and unconcerned about serving the other person. These people may lack mercy and grace and often focus on their partner's faults instead of being accountable for his/her own. This can quickly turn into an abusive relationship where the other party will walk on eggshells to please their partner to keep the peace. Relationships that God has put together are reciprocal, not one-sided.

Also, remember you're not looking for a God to worship. You're looking for a lifetime friend to do life with who's got you the way you've got them. Don't settle for selfish. If you're in a relationship with this type of person, get out right away. This type of relationship can really trip up your thinking and can make you feel guilty for standing up for yourself and wanting what God has for you.

I don't know if there is any greater pain than doing the right thing and getting the wrong result:

However, you must keep doing what's right. Martin Luther King, Jr. was jailed for fighting racism and domestic terrorism. Nelson Mandela was sent to prison for fighting apartheid in South Africa, and Jesus Christ was, of course, crucified for the sins of the world even though He was innocent. History shows us that most of our suffering has some purpose, and those who suffer for doing well usually help create the greatest change. If you're suffering for doing what's right, be encouraged; God is developing you and will probably use you to affect great change on Earth. So, keep going. Living life for the glory of God as a single believer; requires some suffering. Don't decide to quit when it gets rough. Shift your thinking toward God's greater purpose in it. Continue to draw closer to him.

Don't give guys a pass when it comes to guarding your heart just because they're Christians:

Hold your standard even firmer and protect your heart diligently. Often, we tend to think that when dating a Christian man, we don't have to guard our hearts as much. However, doing so is still our responsibility. Just because a man is Christian doesn't mean he's mature, and fellas, a woman being a Christian or a virgin doesn't make her mature, nor does it mean she knows how to carry herself. You must be accountable for shielding your own heart and keeping your value and self-worth high.

Guard your heart above all else, for it determines the course of your life. - Proverbs 4:23 (NLT)

Be willing to let Go When Necessary:

Be okay with taking a perceived loss to maintain your God-given standard. When you're willing to suffer to keep your values, you know that they have become a part of your character. People who have developed in this way will do well at marriage. They will be made ready to accept their inheritance in Christ. Your apparent loss will not be in vain.

"Now if we are children, then we are heirs—heirs of God and co-heirs with Christ, if indeed we share in his sufferings in order that we may also share in his glory." - *Romans 8:17* (NIV)

Don't maintain a loss mindset

Even though you'll be required to experience some losses and go through them while trusting God, you don't want to develop a mindset of loss, less than, or doing without. People who develop this way of thinking often make poor choices to avoid future loss. They may not realize that not having certain things and shifting our focus can be beneficial because it causes us to depend on God more, which builds our faith and allows for miracles and overflow.

In 2017, God spoke into my spirit, telling me not to look at myself based on what I don't have, but from what I do have. When we do focus on what we think we don't have, we avoid fully living our lives, trying to make up for what we're "missing." If I'd focused on the latter, for example, I might have felt that since I'd never been married, I should do whatever it takes to get there. Or because I haven't experienced romantic love, I could settle for anything that seems loving. A mindset of loss is based on the fear of not having enough and not trusting God. Thus, we feel we have to make up for what we lack. This is not God. Instead, we should focus on what we have now and remember that God has brought us this far and know He will complete what he has started. We must consistently renew our minds and expect what God has promised us as his sons and daughters.

"So you have not received a spirit that makes you fearful slaves. Instead, you received God's Spirit when he adopted you as his own children. Now we call him, 'Abba, Father.'" - *Romans 8:15* (NIV)

God doesn't want us to see ourselves as slaves, who aren't a part of the family, not anticipating our inheritance. He wants us to see ourselves as assured, bold, and confident in our standing as His sons and daughters. Children are guaranteed an inheritance from their fathers; thus, we shouldn't even have a concept of lack. When God calls us out of this mindset, He's calling us out of the fear of servanthood. Servants do necessary work but aren't guaranteed an inheritance of their masters. Many women and men of God have been obedient and haven't seen it pay off immediately. The enemy wants us to be afraid that our work will never pay off and that things will always be the same. God, however, wants to assure us that the amount of work we do doesn't matter. He's providing us an inheritance based on us being his children, not on our works.

How I renew my mind against developing a mindset of loss:

I meditate on and speak the Word of God concerning loss; Joel 2:23-26 are some of the main verses I use. In those scriptures, God promises to repay Israel for what they'd lost in their harvest due to swarms of locust and various insects. God re-affirms His faithfulness to His people, letting them know they will experience overflow. I consistently speak this passage over my life and reflect on it. I also meditate on the scripture of the five loaves of bread and two fish. It appeared there wouldn't be enough to feed the entire crowd, but Jesus multiplied what was there, producing more than enough.

I read and contemplate these scriptures to re-wire my thinking so I'm not focusing on what I see and how things appear, but on God being able to do the miraculous in my life and provide a godly spouse, no matter how it looks. This shift helps me continuously rest in God while I expect His promise.

Virginity does not assure great sex after marriage:

Recently, I've seen a few stories popping up from blogs and online magazines about virgins who waited until marriage and ended up unsatisfied sexually. Virginity is not something you can trade in for great sex. We all need to choose someone we've cultivated a safe, secure, strong, emotional, spiritual, and intellectual relationship with. If we don't decide on a person who's willing to wholly invest in a relationship, then yes, the bedroom activities may be lacking.

I once dated a guy who claimed to respect my desire to wait for sex until marriage, but he was very selfish and expected me to toss my values because he "worked for it" by paying for our dates. He pushed to have an intimate connection physically instead of building it mentally, spiritually and emotionally. Even though he and I had never been sexually intimate, I realized that if we had at some point, it wouldn't have been that good. Why? Because he was selfish. It was something he acknowledged as a flaw but didn't make any effort to change while we were dating.

The truth is a person who tries to force a connection by jumping straight to the physical instead of forming intimacy in other aspects may very well not consider the sexual, emotional, or other needs of his spouse during marriage because his aim was about pleasing himself instead of God and his wife. We have to stop thinking that sex will be great after marriage simply because of the act. To have great sex, a marriage needs two individuals who are genuinely committed to the well-being of each other as individuals. Selfishness and disregarding the other person is almost a sure sign that a marriage will have a bad sex life. This is something that should be discussed and observed, to some degree, prior to tying the knot. We must also apply discernment. Are we being selfish in holding on to someone who isn't for us that may mesh better with someone else?

One of the greatest lessons I've learned is that everyone isn't for me. There will likely be someone else out there who will match a selfish person, for example, but it shouldn't be you. Don't try to make someone who's not on your level be with you. By doing this, you may have to force other aspects of the relationship, including sex in the marriage. Forcing sex in a relationship to keep it together will eventually get old. We have to have more than that to build on.

It's far better to have a safe, committed environment cultivated by both spouses who consider each other as they learn each other's bodies within the marriage bed, which is undefiled. Both parties should agree to please one another. The environment should be so safe that open communication about sex should be the norm. This can only happen when aspects outside of a physical connection were worked on while the couple was single, dating, courting, and within the marriage.

Christians, don't quit the wait in the middle

When a person decides to stop waiting for sex until marriage because they think it's not paying off that person will need to question their motives for waiting. Were you doing it only to be rewarded with a spouse? That's an empty motivation. We should delay sex out of simple obedience to God. In the Bible, God says those that love Him will keep His commandments. We should seek to obey Him because we love Him. A woman who only waits because of what others think, or because she believes she'll be rewarded a man, or to gain some sort of notoriety has got it twisted. The wait won't be easy; as a matter of fact, it will be extremely hard. You'll face rejection, self-doubt, and others putting you down because they'll think that you think you're better than them. A person waiting for the wrong reasons may not be able to endure all of this. However, a person who loves God will. Remember, love endures all and always hopes for the best. Loving God deeply will allow you to wait all the way until the end. Focus on building that quality, intimate relationship with the Lord where you learn to love Him more than your desires for romantic love. Besides, there is no love greater than His anyhow.

Forgive your parents for what they didn't give you:

Some of us didn't grow up with a solid identity from our parents. Instead, we may have had various curses spoken over us. Some missed out on knowing either one or both of their parents. Satan uses what we lacked from our parents to trap us in the same bondages that they were in, but we have to break the cycle. In psychology, there is something called a self-fulfilling prophecy, where people act out the behaviors spoken over them. This is a tool the enemy uses, especially when it's an authority figure. It can be a struggle, even in adulthood, to become the real you when you're fighting the curses that were spoken over you as a child and even as an adult.

Breaking free from the toxicity from our parents requires us to be thankful for what we did get from our parents and deal with our subconscious void that drives us to attempt to fix what we missed out on as youth. We must become responsible and whole adults to stop the negative cycles. The truth is, many of our parents were broken, and some of them still are. In their generation, they didn't have ample access to the same wisdom, knowledge, and revelation we do now. Thus, they require a whole other level of grace. When we give them this grace and forgiveness, many of us will be free, and we'll begin moving forward. Generation Y and Z have a greater responsibility to heal because of our access to knowledge and wisdom. We have to do better. We have to break the cycle. We cannot use the excuses of the past any longer. To whom much is given, much is required. Our parents aren't God; they could only give what they had.

"Like a fluttering sparrow or a darting swallow, an undeserved curse does not come to rest." - Proverbs 26:2 (NIV)

"Like a fluttering sparrow or a darting swallow, an undeserved curse will not land on its intended victim." - Proverbs 26:2 (NLT)

The above scripture suggests that we have a choice. We don't have to be in agreement with the curses spoken over our lives. Anything declared against us will find no rest if we don't align ourselves with it. Again, we have a choice. We can say, "The curse in my family stops with me, and it will not continue." Just as the bird flying in the air with no place to rest, don't give negative words or cycles a resting place in your life. Instead, forgive, speak and act out the Word of God over your life, and it will have no power over you. This is a necessary part of healing and wholeness before entering a relationship. You can do this!

Some People Say, "I love hard."

This is often used as a reason why someone shouldn't take our love for granted, but it's better to love smart first, then love hard. Even the Bible says not to cast your pearls before swine. In other words, don't give your valuable love to someone who can't appreciate it.

Never beg anyone to love you:

If you have to plead with someone to love you, more than likely, they won't be willing to put in the necessary work for the relationship to work. They'll be quicker to give up because they weren't that committed in the first place. Wait for the one who values being with you. You're worth it.

Don't lower your standard because no one has appreciated it yet:

That person will come. You gotta still be you the way God intended you to be. Resolve any temptation to lower your standard before dating/courting someone. Pray for God to send you people like Him, who are committed to holiness so you can encourage each other.

Always carry yourself with the utmost respect no matter who is offended:

    Only a person with ill intentions will be offended by someone respecting themselves. Some people who are interested in dating us will test us to see how far we're willing to let them go. I don't care if you think a person will leave you alone or treat you wrong if you don't give in, always respect yourself. When you choose to disrespect yourself, you're showing others it's okay for them to do the same. At the end of the day, some of the guys interested in me were disappointed, but they could only respect me because of how I treated myself. Don't apologize for respecting yourself; the right person will love that about you.

BOOK INFORMATION/SOCIAL MEDIA INFORMATION

"The Single Christian Woman's Guide": Wisdom in Getting to Our God Ordained Man of Promise

"The Wholeness Action Plan"

www.intercession4ageneration.org
www.Russelynwilliams.com
Available at all major online retailers

	Intercession For A Generation
	**@intercession4ag**
	**@intercession4ag**
	Intercession For A Generation
 **BLOG - Life & Relationship Lessons**	www.intercession4ageneration.org www.Russelynwilliams.com

www.ingramcontent.com/pod-product-compliance
Lightning Source LLC
Chambersburg PA
CBHW052102070526
44584CB00017B/2305